High Heels
and
Headdresses

High Heels *and* Headaddresses

Memoirs of a Vintage Vegas Showgirl

Betty Bunch

LifeStories Books • Las Vegas, Nevada

All photographs courtesy of the author unless otherwise noted.

Editor: Ginger Meurer
Book Designer: Joe da Costa
Production Coordinator: Stacey Fott

Library of Congress Cataloging in Publication
Bunch, Betty.
    High heels and headdresses : memoirs of a vintage Vegas showgirl / Betty Bunch.
    244 p. : photos ; 23 cm.
Bunch relates the story of her life, and her many years as a showgirl in various Las Vegas shows.
ISBN: 1-935043-58-7
ISBN-13: 978-1-935043-58-4

1. Dancers—Biography. 2. Showgirls—Biography. 3. Bunch, Betty. 4. Las Vegas (Nev.)—Social life and customs. I. Title.
792.78'092 [B] dc-22   2011   2011930773

ISBN -13: 978-1-935943-58-4 (pbk)
ISBN -13: 978-1-935043-59-1 (e-book)

An imprint of Stephens Press, LLC
1111 West Bonanza Road ~ Las Vegas, Nevada 89106
www.stephenspress.com ~ www.lifestoriesbooks.com

Printed in United States of America

Dedication

This book is dedicated to:

My earthly son Rick Rosenthal for his enthusiasm, support and love. Wow, he is good looking! And to his beautiful wife, Terri. Terri, thanks for always bailing me out of computer problems. My heavenly son, Dan Rosenthal (1970-2010) for being my spiritual advisor and the world's sweetest child. Phylis Noblett, who started all this. It is all her fault!

A special appreciation to my mentor, the brilliant Geoff Schumacher, who made me write it down. Dr. Mary Schramski, who would not let me quit writing it down. To Joyce Marshall-Moore, curator of UNLV Special Collections. Alice, you are the dearest sister a girl could have.

And thanks to the staff at the *Review-Journal's View Newspapers*, publishers of my monthly *Vintage Vegas* column. They are magnificent.

Contents

Preface

Working as a professional dancer, is trivia wise, replete with over-the-top impossibly romantic stories and legends such as the classic "chorus dancer takes over for star, becomes star herself" or "millionaire falls in love with blond chorus girl," or "girl in sweater discovered in drugstore, becomes a star."

Life upon the wicked stage seems very attractive to little nobodies from nowhere. Certainly it did to me.

Of course you are now waiting for me to add, "But it's very difficult hard work." True. Too, too, true.

But guess what, several of those legendary situations actually happened to me; only I was just too dumb to take advantage of them.

The biggest agent in Hollywood tapped me on the shoulder while I was doing *The Twist* in front of the Louis Prima band at Ciro's in Beverly Hills, handed me his card, and said "Call me in the morning. I want you to do *The Twist* with my client, Edd "Kookie" Brynes, on *77 Sunset Strip*. You'll have three lines and get your SAG card."

I did call him, I did do the show, and I did get the card (actually, I was Taft-Hartlied), but left Los Angeles for Las Vegas to do the Louis Prima Show at the Desert Inn, and never called the agent again. That's dumb.

While at the Desert Inn, a millionaire fell in love with me and financed acting school back in Los Angeles after the show was over. If you're thinking he must have been more than a friend, you'd be wrong. But his pals at the Santa Anita race track thought I was his girlfriend, and that's all he cared about. He was a very sweet (though boring) white-haired gentleman who looked exactly like my grand-father, maternal side. He gave me the creeps. He also gave me a full-length fur coat for the holidays, a white sheared beaver. Shecky Greene called me "white coat" all that winter at the Riviera. As in, "Oh, there's white coat now."

Being a dancer in Las Vegas wasn't just about the perks. It was about witnessing history. I feel so sorry for everybody who never got to see Judy Garland sit on the edge of the New Frontier stage and sing her heart out right in front of you, or the one and only Frank Sinatra hold you in the palm of his hand twenty feet away at the Sands, or Jimmy Durante knock your socks off right under your nose (or under his nose I should say) at the Desert Inn, or Liberace amaze you with his music at the Riviera, or Dean Martin take your breath away at the Sands, or Barbra Streisand raise the hair on your arms at the Riviera, or Sammy Davis Jr. do all the above wherever he played. I'm sorry for those who missed too many other great stars in intimate venues to name here. Don't get me started on the lounges. I miss it all.

With Donald O'Connor

Chapter 1

I Am A Gypsy

*D*ancers have to go where the work is, so we are called gypsies in the business. We go from stage (Equity), to movies (Screen Actors Guild), to nightclubs (American Guild of Variety Artists), to TV (American Federation of Television and Radio Artists), and back again.

More than fifty years ago, this gypsy was into my fifth week of work as a Moro-Landis Dancer at the Sahara Hotel on the Strip in Las Vegas. I'd been hired December 10, 1955, for the Donald O'Connor Show, in Los Angeles, where we rehearsed for a week without Donald, then drove individually to Las Vegas, down that long two-lane highway, now Interstate 15, across the big empty Mojave Desert, past a wide place in the road called Baker. I held my breath up the Baker grade, hoping my 1949 Dodge wouldn't overheat. The December cool saved us, us being me and another dancer who needed a ride. I was glad to have help with gas. Mark was to join me within a week by bus.

We stopped in Barstow for gas and cottage cheese. They had dates for sale. Dates grew in this place! On down the road, seven hours after we'd left L.A., we spotted those bright lights in the near distance and I was hooked forever on Vegas. The view coming down that last downgrade into the Las Vegas Valley still gives me goose bumps just as it did that evening. It was twilight, *l'heure bleue*, my favorite time.

Slightly revived by the excitement of actually seeing our destination, we passed a few nondescript motels, a few bars, then suddenly Highway 101 was the Strip. Huge on our left sat the Dunes, all white, with a big porte cochere in front and a great big sultan with turquoise turban, arms akimbo, standing on the roof. Quickly, on the right was the Flamingo, set far back from the highway with lots of green manicured lawns and pink lights with a huge marquee that said, "Now appearing, Tony Martin." Next we passed the Sands, its huge marquee said, "Lena Horne with Freddy Bell and the Bellboys in the Sands Lounge! " We passed a couple of blocks of motels and desert, then the Royal Nevada on the left, jammed up next to the Stardust with its huge, incredible sign. Then, on the right, the Riviera, five stories tall, the only high-rise on the strip and they had Jimmy Durante in the showroom! Two more blocks of desert, and then we spotted three plaster camels on the lawn, and OUR hotel, the Sahara, on the right, across the street from the El Rancho, starring Sophie Tucker in the showroom. Those two were on the corner of San Francisco Street, now called Sahara Avenue, and the Strip. The place we'd been directed to was another two blocks, then left on Cincinnati Street to a newish very nice motel on the right.

Next morning we made it to rehearsal at 10 a.m. in the Congo Room of the most exciting place this little Texas rube had ever seen: elegantly dressed people, sparkling crystal light-fixtures, the jangle of real silver dollars falling out of slot machines, the quiet hum of blackjack tables, shouting and laughter coming from the craps tables and the bar. There was a party going on and money was all over the place. I'd never seen nor imagined anything like it, not even in a movie.

Only three of us were new. The other gypsies were experienced and only one or two were at all friendly to the newcomers. But George Moro was like a kindly uncle and Donald O'Connor was incredibly handsome and friendly. He immediately joined a little group of us to say "Good morning, ladies, everybody OK?"

One of the old-hand girls said, "You have the most beautiful teeth Mr. O'Connor."

He said, "Call me Donald. My teeth are all porcelain caps and took hours in the dentist's chair. But thanks."

Louie Depron, the famous Hollywood choreographer was there as Donald's coach, along with Sidney Miller, who was also in the show, a wonderful comedian. Mr. Depron had invented the Depron Shuffle, a very difficult advanced tap move done with the side of the foot requiring a lighting fast flip-snap of the ankle that made a rat-ta-tat-tat sound in one count. Donald did it effortlessly.

Tap was my thing, I was considered expert, taught advanced tap in my hometown, Austin, Texas, but I couldn't do that darn Depron Shuffle. Neither could anyone else, except Donald of course. Fortunately, it wasn't in our routine, we just played with it, having fun. No worries.

Then we were informed that our entrance was to be a terrifying slide down a nine-and-a-half foot metal slide, undoubtedly from a child's play set after we appeared on a ten-foot tall platform that stretched across the stage. We had to slide down standing up and holding a pose, in our slippery tap shoes with two inch heels, then leap off at the bottom and flap-ball-change to positions on the stage with Donald.

We were doing a great routine to "42nd Street" with Donald in all-white tails and top hat and us in all black tails and trunks and top hats.

Opening night, December 28, 1955, Donald left his front center star position and came back to page each one of us down that slide, presenting each of us while at the same time giving us a close hand we could grab if necessary. He knew how scared we were, me especially, since it was my first big-time professional job. Working as an act, no-one knew if I made a mistake except me. In chorus dancing one tiny mistake sticks out and is noticed by everybody.

I've never before or since met a star who was as considerate and giving as Donald O'Connor. (Well maybe Tony Martin) Thirty or so years later, we elected Donald President of our Professional Dancers Society. He also sent each one of us a dozen American Beauty roses that opening night. I was thrilled beyond words. My cheeks were sore from smiling and grinning. I wiggled like a Cocker Spaniel for days. And I had done the slide perfectly.

Three exciting weeks later on closing night, Donald invited us all and our dates to dinner at the Alpine Village after the midnight show. The buffet in the private dining room had an apple-in-mouth roasted pig, the first I'd ever seen. It was delicious, as my life should have been at that point: a lifelong dream realized and a handsome husband who loved me.

However, the truth was, Mark was unable to get a job, as the Musicians Union required a six-month waiting period, and he had taken to staying out all night and returning home drunk as a skunk and smelling like one, at dawn. Further, he almost never wanted to make love, which I had decided I liked a lot. Cuddling and caring was important to me. What on earth could be wrong? Had I suddenly turned unattractive? Apparently yes. It must be my fault. I was a very sad little girl. I actually wondered if maybe I smelled bad and took to showering twice a day and gargling mouthwash.

Mark often stopped by rehearsal and chatted with us on breaks or joined us on longer lunch breaks in the coffee shop. He made friends with some of the girls, but other of the girls made subtle fun of him in the dressing room. "So has your husband found work yet Betty, or is he still working as a busboy at the Silver Slipper?"

He had found that job and I felt he was doing the best he could. I didn't know how to handle the bitches who patronized me like that.

It took me years to learn how to handle that kind of girl. Even then I always resolved not to treat them in kind. I wouldn't lower myself to that level.

I think my little weight problem actually stems from that extremely vulnerable time in my youth. It just so happened that most of the other eleven girls were on the beefy side. Two of them, sisters, had especially large thighs, so they were referred to as "the Ham Sisters" by my cattily observant husband. We wore flesh-colored net hose, in which their thighs reminded him of the meat counter at Easter.

I on the contrary was steadily losing weight. We danced extremely hard, typically four hours of daily rehearsal learning the next show followed by two shows a night with the current star, no nights off.

We worked seven days per week. If you got sick or hurt and had to miss a show, your paycheck was docked accordingly. If you did that often, you were fired. We had no insurance. After opening night with the new star, we got the next week off from rehearsal. I personally worked ten months without a night off and only got one then because the entire line was let go.

But heavy exercise wasn't why I was losing weight. The real reason was that I had finally realized that my darling husband was gay.

Before we married he had said to me, "Betty, you do know that I'm gay don't you?"

But I didn't know exactly what that meant. I thought it had to do with boys playing dirty games like writing their names in the snow, or "you show me yours, etc." With my Victorian upbringing and no males around, I simply didn't know anything about sex except that it was bad.

And there had never been a divorce in my family. It was the fifties and divorce was neither done nor talked about, much less "gay," what on earth could that be? Horrible words from the Bible hovered in the background, but that was unthinkable.

So I stopped eating. I loved my Marky. He was the big brother/ best friend I'd always lacked and wanted. And when he got around to it, he could be wonderfully sexy. His big shoulders and hands and bronzed muscles turned me on. And he was gentle and sweet and romantic.

He was also German and fancied himself as the chef of the house. And I appreciated his efforts to have a meal prepared when I got home from rehearsal, but heavy pot roast with mashed potatoes and gravy in the 104 degree Mojave Desert summer made my stomach rebel, so the weight just fell off.

One payday Saturday night, our line-captain, a nice person when sober, handed me my check and said sternly, "Come with me."

In my lucky pink, very short robe, net stockings, and high-heels, she marched me down the back stairs to the kitchen and with the dishwashers, busboys, and waiters watching, made me crawl up and sit on the meat scale. At just under five feet eight inches, I weighed 117 pounds.

"I've made a note of that," she said. "If you lose any more weight, we'll have to let you go. You're making the other girls look fat."

The other girls, nearly all friends now, kindly started feeding me beer instead of my usual soda water between and after the shows, or there was banana cream pie in the coffee shop or across the street at Foxey's during lunch break at rehearsals.

So I didn't lose any more weight then, nor indeed ever again. I've always blamed that line captain for my lost movie star career. Every lady movie star I've ever met was excruciatingly thin. The world of professional performing has a one-track mind for women: looks, looks, looks. But one of the singular charms of show business is the indifference we denizens feel toward anything except looks and talent. We don't care about your color, your faith, your pocketbook, your background, your education or anything except your talent. Oddly, looks are considered a talent. Like a really gorgeous girl, who can nether dance nor sing nor act, is still spoken of as talent.

With Jimmy Durante

Chapter 2

Wills Point, Texas

*W*ills Point, Texas, where I was born in 1934, is sixty miles east of Dallas, just a whistle stop back then, but considered a chic place to live now. My Daddy's barber shop was one of the short block of small stores lined up on each side of the railroad track. Mother had retired from teaching English, and my sister Alice was eighteen months older than I. We lived in a small white board house two blocks from the railroad. The house had a huge Mulberry tree in front. I remember the delicious hot-from-the-sidewalk mulberries, and the purple fingers they produced.

The first story told about me that I can remember was that one afternoon an old tramp came into the small grocery store on that strip of shops with me in his arms, dressed in a diaper. Me, not the tramp. The big recession was on and there were copious tramps around.

"Does anybody know whose baby this is?" he asked. "I found her just now walking down the middle of the railroad tracks about a quarter mile out of town."

"I think that may be Chester Bunch's baby," somebody said. "His barber shop is two stores down."

The tramp brought me to Daddy. They said I wasn't crying. I seemed happy enough being carried around by the strange man. I was sixteen months old.

I see this story as a metaphor of my entire life so far. I'm always chasing rainbows and adventures, running away from nap time and restraints straight into danger, being rescued by some man who turns out to be out of work, a perfectly happy girl none-the-less, expecting ice cream to be delivered by my daddy, if only I could find him.

I've always loved the old folk song, "Oh don't you see that lonesome dove that flies from vine to vine. He's searching for his own true love as I have searched for mine." And ice cream.

Daddy joined the army in 1917, right before his eighteenth birthday. He wanted to fight the Germans. He played the piano in the company's jazz band. He was six foot two inches. When Grandfather Bunch's first in Parker County Packard Sedan got a flat tire, my grandmother said, "Well, let Chester pick up the front bumper so you can change it."

And he did. My Grandfather Bunch was a farmer, cotton-broker and postmaster.

Daddy had nine redheaded sisters and one brother. My hair is auburn, it photographs as dark brown but in sunlight was distinctly red. Mother always denied that I was a redhead. Her pet name for me was her "little black-haired baby."

When I was seven months old and Mother was planning to take us home to her parents for Christmas, my sister Alice found Daddy's barber scissors and cut my curls off in chunks, some down to the scalp. Mother saved those curls and I found them in an envelope marked *Betty's Baby Hair*. They are absolutely red. Being "treated like a redheaded stepchild" is a Southern expression indicating scorn. I don't know why she denied what I was.

I think all this disapproval and rejection was decidedly a factor in my success as a dancer and actress. The first thing you have to learn as a performer is how to handle rejection. I was an expert, had handled it for all the years of my childhood. You can't go home again; you just go on to the next audition.

My father was a very sweet and grateful man. For years after the tramp brought me back, Daddy always insisted all tramps be fed a hot meal from our kitchen. After we moved to Austin, we were a "marked house," meaning our address and directions to it were posted down by the railroad tracks in chalk on a wall somewhere. There was a steady stream, I'd say one a week, of homeless men knocking on our back door asking if there was any work they could do for a meal. If Mother was home, she'd have them do some yard work. But by 1940, Daddy had developed early onset Parkinson's disease. He was forty years old.

When they first found out Daddy's diagnosis, that there was no cure, and that he would probably live another twenty-plus years, paralyzed and needing expensive care and medicines, Mother started going to work with Daddy every day, bought the salon from the owner, and learned the hairdressing business. Mother was the eldest of six siblings and could excel at anything. When she was a teacher, she became a principal very quickly.

Doctors traced the Parkinson's to Daddy's having the Spanish flu with a very high temperature in the pandemic of 1918. The whole army camp was ill. No one took care of them as everybody was sick. More than a few died. The Parkinson's disease took twenty-two years to develop. Daddy slowly stayed home more and more. By 1946, he was home in a hospital bed, unable to work, barely able to walk. I was his walk starter. I knew exactly how hard to push on his back to get him off balance enough to start walking. I was also his masseuse as his arms and legs hurt from lying in bed. And I was the only one besides Mother who could understand what he was trying to say. If we were out in public, people stared. Daddy looked and walked like Frankenstein. I also fed him, because it was so hard for him to do it for himself.

Mother bought a house in 1941 before the war. The first piece of furniture we had was a piano. Alice and I took piano lessons. Mother arranged a private recital after we had studied a little over a year. She made beautiful long taffeta dresses and served cake and punch to relatives and friends on a Sunday afternoon in our living room. Alice also took voice. I took ballet and tap and then dropped piano because our teacher told Mother I didn't know one note from another and was playing entirely by ear, so I was a waste of time and money.

We were required to listen to *The Bell Telephone Hour* on Saturday mornings while our friends got to listen to *The Shadow Knows* and *The Lone Ranger*. I still prefer classical music, especially the *William Tell Overture*.

We had a full time housekeeper, Myrtle, (a saint if ever there was one), who took care of Daddy all day, gave him lunch, and made dinner for all of us as well as keeping the house spotless, laundry and all. She might have weighed ninety-five pounds soaking wet. After Alice and I were grown, Mother paid for Myrtle's daughter to go to business school.

On one occasion, Myrtle was with Mother and me driving up to the Veterans Administration Hospital in Temple, Texas. We had to take Daddy there when we could no longer turn or bathe him. We stopped to eat and Mother told me to wait in the car a minute. Myrtle disappeared. When Mother returned to the car, she explained that she had arranged for Myrtle to be fed in the kitchen of the little roadside diner. I had a fit, refused to come inside and eat without Myrtle, and cried, refusing to get out of the car. Mother got stern, said, "Baby, that's the way it is, now come inside and have your lunch. There's nothing you can do. "When we went in, I saw the sign posted over the entrance door. Later, when I got a degree in American studies, we learned that black people especially hate whites who realized how awful blacks were treated and did nothing.

Mother was extremely strict, more so than other mothers according to my girlfriends from that time. Despite having Myrtle, we were required to make our beds and do our own ironing. Mother said we weren't allowed to be rebellious like other normal teenagers because we had an invalid father and she didn't have time or energy to cope with nonsense because she had to make a living. We had to toe the line.

One early Sunday morning, Mother shook me awake and said, "Please come with me baby, I have to go see Daddy and it's raining and I don't want to go alone."

On the two-hour trip, she said the air-conditioning in the beauty shop, the Majestic, had gone out. She'd already seen her banker and gotten a loan, but the papers required Daddy's signature. He owned the beauty shop. When we got to the hospital, she put a pen in Daddy's hand and guided it in a signature. I became a feminist then and there. Had it been me, I would have forged his signature.

Daddy had been a "white suiter," a phrase referring to the early hairdressers who started as barbers, cut Flappers hair into bobs, realized hairdressing was a new up and coming business, and invested in it. The custom of the time in fancy salons was for the owner to wear a white suit, shirt, and tie, and step in after an underling did the shampoo, to perform the cut and styling. In the small towns around Dallas in the twenties, Daddy sent an advance man ahead to post notices that Mr. Chester, guest artist at a local shop, would be seeing appointments for the very latest thing, permanents including personalized cut and style. He went to Granbury, Eastland, Denton, Weatherford, Dennis, and more and was very successful, until 1929, that is. One week in the thirties his barber shop in Canton took in 50 cents.

When I was three, Mother and Daddy moved down to Austin to be close to Bigmother and Bigdaddy, Mother's parents, who had moved there earlier to seek better opportunity.

My grandfather got a job at the State Capitol building as an engineer, a euphemism for a versatile "can do" employee. That famous building looks just like the one in Washington, D.C. It's domed and built in Texas granite. He mostly ran the generator that kept the lights on, but when it was found that he had been a farmer in Van Zandt County, they asked him to plant a large shipment of trees anywhere he pleased on the grounds. So my grandfather was responsible for the famous column of oak trees on each side of the long sidewalk promenade leading up to the Capitol steps. They are huge now, a real Austin landmark.

Everybody has a sob story about their childhood. Mine is that I started first grade (Texas had no kindergarten) when I was only five years and three months old, so was always "the baby" and therefore the outcast. My neighborhood had four girls in my class nearby, and we all walked to school together. But one Saturday morning when I was thirteen, and they were fourteen and fifteen, I walked to the library and was standing on the corner walking back home, when the other four girls, my gang, drove by, with one of their mothers at the wheel. They elaborately pretended not to see me, screaming with laughter, hanging out the car windows pointing at imaginary things in the sky, so as not to be looking at the corner where I stood, not invited to go to the movies with them. They knew from sleepovers that I still wet the bed, didn't have periods or wear a bra yet, and thought liking boys was silly.

For so long, Daddy was sick and couldn't talk. Mother went to work running a business in high heels ten to twelve hours a day and was exhausted and cross when she got home. My big sister, whom I adored, hated me from the day I was born and literally did not speak to me for months at a time. My classmates rejected me as "just a baby." I became a loner, a lifelong condition I'm used to now. It gives me time to read.

With my sister Alice

Chapter 3

Getting Started

I joined the Austin Civic Theatre when I was fourteen, and started doing my little tap routines during the entr'actes between acts of the melodramas that were standard fare then.

Organizations started asking me to perform at their luncheons, like the Rotary Club, the Optimists, the Lions, etc. They usually paid $5. I always handed the money directly to Mother, who made much of the fact that we didn't have a working father and she was struggling to make ends meet so we wouldn't have to sleep on the street.

Then there were the weekend sing-a-longs, with special guests (such as me!) at Zilker Park, Austin's beautiful grassy natural amphitheater at Barton Springs. The hillside was always covered with 300 or so people on Saturday nights. I did those performances for free, but I loved the applause.

At fourteen or fifteen, I did a small role at the Austin Civic Theatre, and was directed by Mel Pape, a wonderfully kind and knowledgeable teacher and director of the Austin Civic Theatre organization, who taught me basic stage acting. He taught me well. Due to his teaching, I got the lead in my senior play with the Red Dragons at Austin High School. Mel later became Jackie Gleason's right-hand man. I'm still in touch with Mavis Pape, his wonderful wife.

After my sophomore year at the University of Texas majoring in drama, with an emphasis in dance, a man I knew from the Austin Civic Theatre hired me for a summer project he produced, a production of *The Drunkard*, the great classic melodrama that was to play the Ruidoso Hotel in Ruidoso, New Mexico, for the summer of 1953. I was hired as Little Nell, but in classic Show Business style, the leading lady quit, and Bob (the boss) bumped me up to the lead role, Mary. I already knew the words from rehearsal. One afternoon before we left for Ruidoso, (I rode out with the piano player and his wife) I sat at the back of Hogg Auditorium on the University of Texas campus and recited the entire script to myself just to prove to myself that I could. It was an edited version; the original is three hours long, but still a full-length play. It was wonderful to be young and have a great memory.

The amazing thing about the job was that Bob was paying $50 dollars a week. My sister worked in Austin for $35 per week, and she was a hotshot secretary.

Once we were there the cast was given a list of available rentals, bedroom and bath in private homes for the most part. Mine cost $5 per week. I needed another $5 per week for food, so sent Mother $35 a week, leaving me $5 for walking around money. I was rich!

I am still grateful for that job for all the lessons it taught me. For one thing, the other women in the show were all jealous of me being the star no matter how nice I was to them, but primarily, the best lesson I learned was about money. We always gathered at a certain spot to receive our salary checks at the end of the week. Closing night, end of August, we gathered as usual and Bob said, "You have done a great job everybody, thank you very much. However, I haven't made enough profit to be able to pay you this last check. Sorry," and he turned to go.

Someone said, "But, how will we get home?"

"You'll have to do that the best way you can," Bob said. Then he and his bitch wife hurried out the door. She was one of the jealous ones and had been rude to me. I called Mother, she called an aunt who lived in Midland, the aunt and her husband were just leaving for a vacation and said they would be happy to drive to Ruidoso to pick me up before they drove back to Austin to see her brother, my daddy. So it all worked out. But I became a staunch union supporter on the spot.

I had sent Mother enough to pay for my books and tuition for my junior year, including sorority fees. (I'm a Delta Zeta.) I got a job teaching tap at a dance school close to campus as soon as I got home. It paid enough that I didn't have to ask Mother for money.

At the end of my junior year, Mother broke my heart. She said she couldn't afford to send me to school another year, and that it was time I got a job and helped her take care of Daddy. (Hadn't I always?) Further, she didn't know how much longer she could work; I should be taking care of her, too. (Mother was a dedicated hypochondriac, lived to be ninety-three.) Of course I was familiar with the old Southern custom of the youngest girl staying home and devoting her life to taking care of her elderly parents and becoming an old maid.

What hurt so much was the anger with which she said all this. And the fact that I had paid my own way through that junior year with the money I sent from Ruidosa and the job I took teaching dance. She knew about my lifelong dream, obsession really, of being a dancer. I had always helped take care of Daddy. That was my main job around the house after school, and I had always handed over every dime I made, even baby-sitting money. I was accustomed to being a loner, but now I felt like a motherless child, as well.

I felt that my life was over, but an answer came the next day. A new girl in the drama program, Ann from Dallas, called and invited me to accompany her to New Orleans where she had an aunt with whom we could stay. Ann was from a wealthy family. She drove a new Oldsmobile convertible, and in fact had left the car with me when she flew home for a long weekend. It was bright red and spiffy.

Suddenly I remembered a trip to New Orleans my sister Alice and I made one summer to see our own aunt, who no longer lived there. Our aunt and uncle had taken us to see the French Quarter one night and I had observed tap acts no better than I was, working at least two clubs. So I told Ann I'd love to go. I had a two week pay check coming for about $50 dollars. The dance studio was going on very short hours for the summer anyway.

For the first time in my life, I did a sneaky thing: I packed my tap shoes and one costume at the bottom of my suitcase. I told Mother that Ann and I were going for a little vacation, having worked so hard at school all semester, and that I'd be back in five or six days.

Chatting on the long drive, Ann admitted she hoped to see her friend Scott, another drama major on whom she had a crush. He was going to be in the French Quarter for the summer and had given her a phone number.

I found the New Orleans yellow pages in Ann's aunt's home the first afternoon we were there. I wrote down the theatrical agent's name with the biggest ad and noted the address and phone. I took a deep breath and called, told Bess Grundman that I was new in town on break from school, and was an experienced tap act. She asked me to come see her tomorrow or the next day in her office downtown.

In the meantime Ann had called Scott, and he'd invited us to come for coffee one afternoon. So, the next afternoon, Ann let me off at the proper address on Canal Street and arranged for me to meet her and Scott later in the French Quarter. I dressed in my tan silk suit with brown and white, high-heeled Andrew Geller Spectator pumps and matching small bag, my high school graduation outfit, expensive with short white gloves.

Ms. Grundman was a tough, whiskey voice chain-smoker, but kind. She questioned me closely about my experience. I told her the truth, which was evidently good enough. She booked me on the spot for one week at Keesler Air Force Base in Biloxi, Mississippi, starting in one week. I was to do two shows per night at the Airmans Club, then two shows per night at the Officers' Club to make two weeks. She arranged for me to stay in a reduced-rate room in the employee's wing at the White House Hotel, right on the beach in Biloxi. She also arranged for someone from the Air Force base to pick me up and drive me to work and back every evening.

Ann asked Scott to drive back to Dallas with her since I had a job, and he accepted. They dropped me off at the YWCA right off Canal Street. They wished me good luck and gaily drove off, leaving me with a huge lump in my throat, something I was becoming used to. I marched myself in and inquired about spending the night. Yes, they had a bed in the dorm, $5 dollars per night, shower down the hall.

Two other girls were there, and seemed friendly enough. I stayed there two nights until one of the girls suggested we go find an apartment in the Quarter, which would undoubtedly be less than the $35 a week we were paying for the dorm. That girl was well dressed and well spoken, and we were already friends, so I said great, let's do it. Also, she had already gotten a job as hostess at Diamond Jim Moran's restaurant.

We set off down Bourbon Street from Canal, carrying our suitcases. At 516 Bourbon Street we spotted a sign in the window, room for rent. It was shabby but spacious, bath down the hall, $10 per week. The landlady was sweet and friendly. She opened a door in the room and said that was a small kitchen in a closet. It had a toaster and a hotplate. The fridge was out in the room. After we settled in with our skimpy possessions, I opened the "kitchen" door to spot a huge rat sitting on the counter. I never opened that door again. The bath down the hall had a simple latch/hook inside on the door. We later found out the place was actually primarily a Merchant Seaman's hotel. But that landlady kindly watched us constantly and threatened death to anyone who bothered us. Nobody did. Actually, we hardly ever even saw anyone there.

Money was a bit of a problem. It developed that my roommate's tips were pooled with the waitresses and divided at the end of the week. I was pretty much broke after paying the rent and saving enough to buy the bus ticket to Biloxi for my job the next week. But my roommate "stole" from her own tips one dollar per night, and she was generous enough to share with me. We had a strict budget for the dollar: 25 cents for a pack of cigarettes (half a pack apiece), 25 cents each for a hamburger at the Bourbon Street Diner for dinner, and 10 cents for a cup of coffee for me every morning. That was kind of her, I loved a cup in the morning, and she didn't care for it. Then we spent 5 cents for Doublemint gum to help with the hunger, and saved the remaining 10 cents for two days so we could buy a loaf of bread.

On the appointed date, I walked to the Greyhound station and rode the two hours to Biloxi, got off at the White House Hotel, crossed over the highway to the front entrance, put on my white gloves to go into the lobby (I was dressed in the tan silk suit and spectator heels again), and checked in. I called the number I'd been provided and they sent a car for me to go to rehearsal. I stayed there for the show, in my dressing room. The stage manager brought me a sandwich from the kitchen, free. Working for the Air Force is always wonderful, they feed you and they watched over me, too. I only had one scary incident.

One night after I'd been returned to the hotel and had bathed and gone to bed, there was a soft but long and insistent tapping on my hotel door. I simply played possum and whoever it was finally gave up.

Performing is my thing, so the shows went well. One week later, I reversed the whole trip and arrived back at 516 Bourbon Street with my huge paycheck in hand, $150 I think it was. We were rich!

One afternoon I ran into Mark, one of Scott's roommates that I'd met with Ann when we had coffee with them in the Quarter. He and I hit it off immediately and "took up" with each other, as we say in the South. I told him we had a loaf of bread, he said he had a stick of butter back at his apartment, so we fetched it, came back to my room, and had toast. It was delicious. He manned the toaster, not afraid of the rat. He worked part-time. He was actually my first boyfriend. My shy streak with boys and dance schedule prevented any romance developing in high school. I'd had a rather serious steady boyfriend in Ruidosa, but it was one sided, he wanted to marry me. I wanted to have a career and said so. But I adored Mark immediately, part of it I think a natural panic at the realization that I was all alone in a big bad city. And he was gorgeous.

Mark was very bossy. Once I put on blue jeans to go somewhere with him, and he said, "Oh no. I won't be seen with you in those." I pressed him for why, and he said, "People will think you're lesbian. Lesbians all wear jeans, and there are lots of them here in the French Quarter."

After the Kessler Field job, Ms. Grundman booked me into Prima's 500 as the opening act for a stripper, Valetta. Valetta took one look at me and demanded, "How old are you?" I said 20. She yelled, "She's underage, she can't go out front! " Actually Valetta was very sweet and protective. She cooked steaks for me and Mark one night at her apartment.

After the last show, walking home was a little problem in that I was alone, young and wearing heavy makeup. Cars often swerved, or slowed as the drivers called out, "Where you goin' babe? Come over here."

But I'd made friends with the barkers who worked outside each bar on Bourbon Street, trying to pull in customers. Several of them had said hello, so I stopped and told them who I was, that I danced at Prima's, and that I was going home to my room. So they started "shouting me home," a Creole custom. Each man yelled to the next man on the block, "Betty's comin', Betty's comin' " then watched me walk to the next man. Sweet people.

After four weeks at Prima's, Ms. Grundman didn't have anything. I waited two weeks patiently. Then went in person one afternoon to her office and said, I have to work or I'll have to go home to Austin.

She said, out of the blue, "Can you sing?"

I said, "Yes Ma'am!"

"Let me hear you," she said and I stood up and sang, loud, and patting my foot in time, "I hate to see, the evening sun go down!" "St. Louis Blues." She asked if I had an accompanist. Mark had mentioned just that week that he played the piano, so I said yes again. Believe it or not, she booked me into a bar/lounge in Ft. Walton Beach, Florida, for two weeks, with a two-week option, as a singer. I'd never sung outside my high school choir and First Methodist Church choir. Nor had I heard Mark play. Ah, the chutzpah and desperation of youth.

I found a music store and bought a "bible", a cheat sheet of lead lines and lyrics. Mark and I went to the biggest hotel on Canal Street, and wandered around until we found a piano in a convention room, sat down and practiced. He was very good. I didn't find out until later that he played by ear in the key of F only, so couldn't play bridges which nearly always change keys. Also, F isn't my key. It's nearly always too high for me. Details, details.

We studied the music on the Greyhound all the way to Ft. Walton. There was a motel next door to the bar lounge. I swallowed hard and said, "Guess we'll have to stay together, can't afford two rooms. Am I safe with you?"

He said, "You know you are. I would never scare or hurt you."

They had a room with two double beds. He neither scared nor hurt me, which is why I loved him. He was the only man I ever met who didn't try to get in my pants immediately. I thought it was because he was a gentleman.

We ended up working all summer on the Gulf Coast in Pensacola, Bill's, another club in Biloxi and in Homa, Louisiana. We were always held over for two weeks at least. When things got boring at work, I'd dash to the ladies room, change to a costume and tap dance on top of the bar, or hula on the piano. I bought yardage, needle and thread at the dime store and hand sewed a sarong and covered a bra to match.

I started thinking about school in the fall and taking Mark home to meet my family. Mark said he would work at something if I wanted to go back to school. But, Ms. Grundman, made the decision for me, offering me the best job yet, opening act for Dave "Flat Get It" Gardner at Biloxi's Joe Wright's Palladium, for more money than I'd yet made, $210 per week.

Dave Gardner was always high on something. When he was occasionally sober, he was crazy. Opening night, he came into my dressing room to introduce himself, stood behind me sitting in front of a mirror, unzipped his pants, and tapped my shoulder with his penis. I gasped, he laughed, and left. After that, I stayed away from him. After Dave, Leon Prima and his Orchestra was the next act booked into the Palladium, Mr. Prima knew me of course since I'd worked for him, and asked for me to stay to open for him.

Mark and I bought an old car since we were rich and started talking about marrying. We drove home to Austin nonstop. Mother put together a sweet home wedding. She made the white satin dress, shin length. We married on November 26, 1954. Alice played the wedding march. Daddy, in his best satin pajamas, sat in his lounge chair next to the fireplace. Mark's best friend from New Orleans drove in to be his best man and brought a bottle with him. Mark started drinking early, and we finally drove away to spend the night across town at a motel in South Austin. Mark passed out almost as soon as we got there. I spent my wedding night wearing Wind Song, my new white gown and negligee and crying myself to sleep.

Within the week, we drove to Los Angeles where Mark had a friend who owned a bar and said, "You can always come work for me at the piano bar." Mark also had a friend who said, "You can always stay with me." Mark had a lot of friends from the French Quarter.

We'd only been in L.A. a week when I read about an audition for the Moro-Landis Dancers, drove out to the Valley, and got the job!

Chapter 4

The Silver Tiller

At the Sahara, when the Moro-Landis Dancers were told what our next number was, to be learned for the next star, Frankie Laine, the dancers who had been there for a while all groaned.

"Oh No, not the Silver Tiller! That one almost killed me last year," one of them said.

Tillers are notoriously difficult and exhausting and dreaded in the gypsy business. The name comes from a very popular vaudeville act of six sisters, The Tiller Sisters, who lined up in a row, hands on shoulders and kicked over head repeatedly in unison, now thought of in connection with the Radio City Music Hall Rocketts.

It was actually a tap number. We did five minutes of very energetic tap dancing before the tiller started, so we were already tired and out of breath. The tiller section was a full chorus, that's thirty-two bars, two kicks per bar for a total of sixty-four head-high kicks usually followed by a tag of at least four more kicks. Try jumping up and down while kicking eye-high, knee-straight, sometime. You have to be very young and in perfect condition to do that.

Getting off stage at the end was sometimes hard, because girls behind you on the exit would almost knock you down in their hasty effort to get off stage so they could collapse on the floor. I always used the Texas Aggies trick of bending over from the waist, hands on knees, to open the lungs to full capacity, but you had to be off stage to do that obviously.

Performing the thing wasn't as hard as learning it, because you only had to do it twice per night, but in rehearsal, we did it over and over only being allowed to "mark" it once in a while. Torture.

Mother came out to visit during that rehearsal, sat in the house and cried one afternoon. She said she couldn't bear to see us being made to work that hard.

Sometimes you also had to cope with the girl next to you leaning on your shoulder, a forbidden no-no, but never-the-less done by weaker dancers. At the Moulin Rouge in Hollywood the next year, we did an even longer tiller in the opening number, followed by a run around the backstage to re-enter in front of the curtain and kick traveling/hopping right, all the way across the proscenium. And I had a "leaner" next to me. I begged her to stop that, but she didn't. In fact she loudly protested in the dressing room that she didn't lean. So one desperate night, I placed upside-down straight pins through the shoulder pads on my costume.

When she felt the pins, she snapped around to glare at me, but she also lifted her hand off my shoulder. By the way, she was also one of the patronizing bitches in the dressing room back at the Sahara. Gotcha. Was that sinking to her level? I don't think so.

Chapter 5

Mississippi of the West

I know very well what blind unreasoning prejudice is because I am (was) a chorus girl, a Las Vegas chorus girl at that! Chorus girls are assumed to be gold diggers of little talent and loose morals, an opinion usually held by folks not actually acquainted with a top level chorus dancer. So, that clique isn't true of me and certainly not typical of my mates and I can see the blind unreasoning judgment on your male face fellows, as you say, "Yeah sure, wink, nudge," a reaction that's mostly a result of fantasy and wistful thinking on your part. Back in the sixties, the nurses at Sunrise Hospital were wilder than we were.

Sahara Hotel, 1956, working the Teresa Brewer Show as a Moro-Landis Dancer, one night the line-captain announced that one of the casino bosses wanted to speak to the dancers, and would be here in the dressing room any minute. She had no idea why. This was totally unheard of; no one from the hotel/casino ever came backstage. We had just finished the 8 p.m. show and quickly hung up our costumes and got our robes on.

The suit arrived forthwith and said imperiously, "Girls, pull up your chairs in a circle, I have something important to tell you.

"All right, listen carefully. We have hired a new act for the lounge.

They are a troupe of six black men, The Treniers, who are good enter-tainers and attract crowds we're told, but who also have the reputation of liking white women. So, we want you girls to stay far, far away from them. It's OK to go see their show in the lounge as you usually do. Oh don't worry, they won't be allowed to use the lounge dressing rooms. We are having trailers brought in for the north parking lot. That means they will enter the casino through the north side door, so you girls are to stay completely away from that area.

"Do you understand me? We are not going to have an 'incident' in the Sahara. If we see one of you even talking to one of them, you'll be fired on the spot. Is that clear? We mean it," the suit concluded.

And so I became a witness to the mechanisms of the Mississippi of the West as Las Vegas was called in the fifties and early sixties, and with good reason.

Hotel owners on the strip in 1956 were not only prejudiced they were angry and scared about all their graveyard business leaving the strip and going to the Moulin Rouge on Bonanza Road, the integrated "black" hotel on the west side, meaning on the west side of Union Station where the township of Las Vegas started. Business was going there in droves in 1956 because that's where the fun was, where the great stars both black and white were going after 2 a.m. to party together.

Sammy Davis Jr., Frank Sinatra, Dean Martin, Louie Armstrong, Louis Belson (drummer/husband of Pearl Bailey) were all to be found there along with many Strip musicians and performers, drinking, perform-ing informally, relaxing among friends, gambling, or in Dean's case dealing blackjack. The best jazz in the world played live, for kicks, with vocal comments, right off the casino floor. The Strip musicians all brought their horns.

I actually got to see all that! We heard that even though the place was closed, the former owners were going to have one last night of partying, all comped, to finish off the bar stock. A couple of the other Sahara dancers were going and I met them over there.

We didn't talk about it knowing our bosses wouldn't like us going to another hotel, but go we did. It was so crowded you could hardly walk around. I mean shoulder to shoulder. One of the things I love most about being an entertainer is that we are nonjudgmental; don't care about your color, religion, gender, just about your talent.

Bob Bailey was one of my interviewees when I did an oral history project for my American studies professor at the University of Nevada, Las Vegas, in the seventies. Dr. Bailey was the master of ceremonies for the show at the Moulin Rouge in 1956, and he was also chairman of the Civil Rights Commission in Nevada in 1964, the year the Las Vegas Strip finally integrated, at least officially. He told me nobody knows exactly why that hotel/casino closed after only five/six months. Certainly it wasn't for lack of business. According to Bob, it's likely the banks who financed the venture simply called in the mortgage notes and the hotel had to close. So, why on earth did they call in the notes? It was good money.

This makes perfect sense to us old timers who know that State Senator Floyd Lamb was a major stock holder/owner of Nevada State Bank and could be bribed to OK a loan. It was called a "campaign contribution."

His brother, Sheriff Ralph Lamb, was famously zealous about running off the streetwalkers on the Strip. Again, us old timers know this was because he didn't want competition for what rumor said were his own hookers. So the Lamb brothers, senator and sheriff, were well acquainted with all the Strip hotel owners. If the hotel owners were unhappy, they were happy to do something about it. This is all non-news you understand, water under-the-bridge, folks. Las Vegas has always run on tips, favors, comps, and who you know, still does to a larger degree than corporate mentality of today wants to acknowledge.

Claude Trenier told me they were once playing the lounge at the Last Frontier in the fifties, when a friend of theirs, a beautiful young girl who wanted to be a singer, and was almost white, came to see their show at their invitation. They thought she could "pass" and planned to have her get up and sing. But during their set, two burly security guards came in and forcibly removed her from the audience front row. The Treniers were so heartsick and embarrassed, they couldn't (not wouldn't) continue performing and just wandered into the wings not knowing what to do. Hands were shaking, lips were trembling.

A casino host quickly appeared backstage, a bottle of champagne and paper cups in his hands, and said, "Aw come on fellows, please don't stop playing. We love you guys, you're the best! Here, let's drink to friendship and a toast to good times!"

He poured champagne all around and led them back onto the bandstand to lead them in a toast. They finished the set and the evening as scheduled. The next morning they were fired for drinking on stage.

The Treniers played the Moulin Rouge in Hollywood in 1959 I think it was, when I was dancing there. They invited the entire cast and our husbands and dates over for a barbecue at their parents' big old mansion in Santa Monica where several of them still lived when they weren't on the road. It was one of the nicest, most fun showbiz parties I can remember. They knew how to entertain all right. I also remember being really drunk, Mark driving us home drunk, and getting up two hours later to go to *South Pacific* rehearsal at 20th Century Fox. Thank goodness we just ran the *Honey Bun* number once and then played bridge the rest of the day. Leroy Prinz the choreographer, loved to play. I excused myself and napped in a lounge chair in the corner.

Chapter 6

Bosoms

Breast size is a huge issue for today's showgirls, dancers, and cocktail servers working on the Strip just as it was for my generation back in the sixties. George Kliefkin, MD, was the only doctor on the strip in the fifties-sixties. I first went to him with a bad cold in 1956. He was the dancer's doctor with an office where the large gift shop is now on the northwest corner of Sahara and the Strip. He naturally became a sort of father figure, knew us all by name, and he was famous for writing out a prescription for whatever you asked him for: diet pills (I'm fat), thyroid pills (I'm tired), or, after 1957, birth control pills (I want to dance a few more years). Two girlfriends told me he made house calls for abortions, illegal then. Another friend got hooked on the diet pills, a form of speed, and committed suicide years later.

In 1963 Dr. Kliefkin offered direct silicone shots to the breast, $50 per shot, a series of four or five were usually needed.

I said, "No thanks, I'm off to Japan next week."

He said, "You better plan to get them when you come back Betty, otherwise, you won't be able to get a job. Bosses all over town are demanding their dancers and cocktail servers as well as their showgirls get at least a C-cup, D-cup preferred."

The doctor was right about that, and the problem is still out there. We dancers just used falsies as we always had. This was before dancers were ever topless. Of course, that's no longer true.

This preference for large breasts did not exist for Donn Arden dancers and showgirls. He preferred to follow the French tradition of smallish, perfect breasts on his elegant, graceful, willowy showgirls and dancing showgirls in the *Lido De Paris* at the Stardust. Donn also did the shows at the Desert Inn, with "dressed" showgirls and dancers. *Jubilee!*, another Donn Arden show, is still running at Bally's, Donn's standards enforced now by the also legendary Fluff LeCoque.

Big breasts belong in burlesque, Donn said. Donn had class and demanded the same from his performers. He outlawed blue or green eye shadow, spit curls and breasts that jiggled.

"Tacky, tacky!" I remember his yelling at a new nude soloist, who wasn't actually all that big in the breast. "Stiffen your back! You're jiggling!"

Donn Arden's name and persona are still legendary though he has been gone several years now. My proudest resume item is still that I was a Donn Arden dancer for almost four years at the Moulin Rouge in Hollywood. I adored him and was also terrified of him, a common reaction to his demanding, caustic personality! He was a genius and we recognized that.

Donn described what he wanted on his stage as being breasts that would fit into a champagne glass, meaning the old-fashioned coupe' glass. A sweet young reporter interviewed me a few years back and said, "Betty says Donn Arden wanted showgirl's breasts to fit into a champagne flute." Oops.

Is there a point to any of this excessive drivel about the female form?

Yes. I'm sick and tired of trashy performers/strippers calling themselves dancers. I stood at a ballet barre for years, and majored in dance drama at the University of Texas for three years.

A Donn Arden audition for dancers went on for three days and tested the applicant on all dance techniques: ballet, jazz, modern, perhaps tap, depending on the show. Other choreographers were also this thorough, if not as lengthy as Donn Arden's auditions.

Further, still on my soapbox, it really bothers me to see visible edges on the breast implants of dancers so thin you can also see their ribs. Only Cirque du Soleil seems to hire natural figures, and they are the most successful show producers around. Got a clue anyone?

In my day we were very proud to say, "I'm a dancer, currently performing at the Riviera, or the Desert Inn, or the Aladdin, or whatever." Residents and tourists alike treated dancers with extreme courtesy and respect and admiration. Well, OK, not all the casino bosses. If you dressed well and obviously enjoyed having drinks in the lounge after the show, some bosses made assumptions and tried to turn you out. Yes, I mean they were pimps. Not all of course.

But now, in the 21st Century, when I say, "I used to be a dancer." I have to quickly add, "A real dancer, not topless, not a stripper, not a walking showgirl." Either you can do a double pirouette or you cannot. I can.

While I was in Japan in 1965, Steve Parker (Shirley MacLaine's husband) advised me that better silicone shots were done there, so I had it done in Japan and very inexpensively! Unlike the girls Kliefkin treated with industrial grade silicone, I never had any problems.

Nevertheless, I had most of the material removed in 1994: I got tired of worrying about it.

We still have doctors who opened their practices here in the early sixties who still are in practice now. One of them likes to wag his finger and say, "You shouldn't have done that young lady!" I've always wanted to ask him, if he knew silicone shots were bad, why didn't he form a peer review board and stop Kliefkin? If he didn't know they were bad back then, how can he charge dancers with the responsibility for that knowledge? Jerk.

I breast fed both of my sons and as far as I'm concerned, that's all that is important.

Well, not quite: I was a dancer, dammit, a real dancer.

With Martha Raye

Chapter 7

Legs

Having written about bosoms I need to balance the body parts needed in the dancer/showgirl trade. We didn't, in the old days (before-nudity) need bosoms, we just wore falsies under the costumes. Legs were another matter.

Donn Arden, the legendary director/choreographer, started his auditions by holding a line-up, and requesting we stand legs together, ankles touching so he would not have to waste time with unsuitable legs or height or facial features. He expected the knees, and calves to be able to hold a dime.

I remember a beautiful blond girl whom I knew from dance classes, who was a terrific dancer, especially adept at turns. But when her legs were placed in the above manner, there was a 6 inch gap between her knees. It was hard not to cry when she was inevitably asked to leave before she got to dance a step. It seemed so unfair. Legs can't be faked. Well, short legs can be helped with French cut, meaning high-cut costumes. We see those all the time now on most performers, indeed on most bathing suits. I look terrible in hi-cut bottoms. I'm extremely long legged, have a 32-inch inseam, but am also short-waisted, so I look like a new born colt, ungainly and awkward.

I announced when I was nine years old that I was going to be a dancer when I grew up. I had walked home from school with a classmate who said she was going to tap class at the Austin Athletic Club. I joined her and loved the rhythm and moving to the music.

So Mother sent me to the best dance teacher in town, Melba Stewart Huber. Four years of classes later, Mother said she'd had a bad year at the beauty salon and wasn't going to pay for anymore dance classes.

I'll never forget the thud as my heart dropped through my stomach. I went directly to Melba and asked if I could mop the floor, or answer the phone. She said I could "demonstrate," and was on full scholarship from then on. Thank you forever Melba. Melba was also Miss Austin, as beautiful outside as she was inside.

Mother and the rest of my family, aunts and uncles, tried mightily to talk me out of my dream. "Don't be ridiculous, Betty, you're going to get married and have babies. You're just a little girl from the sticks, what chance would you have?" My uncles made much of the fact that they couldn't pinch Betty, her flesh was firm as marble. I was corn-fed all right.

Mother had a good friend who claimed to be a very sophisticated lady: she'd actually been to New York City, and had actually seen professional dancers at musicals and the ballet. She took me aside I'm sure at Mothers request, and said, "Dear, you can't be a dancer."

"Why not? " I demanded.

"Well, er, your legs dear."

"What's wrong with my legs?"

"Well dear, they are heavy. The dancers I saw in New York all had very slender perfect legs."

I started that very night doing one hundred leg swings over my head, repeated on the other side, holding on to my four poster bed before bedtime. I also practiced standing just so in Melba's mirror and I prayed nightly that I be allowed to be a dancer, despite my flawed legs. The truth is, I simply needed to lose weight and did when I left home. It was baby fat.

I majored in dance drama at the University of Texas for three years, did a summer of theater in Ruidosa, New Mexico, worked as a tap act in New Orleans where I met my husband, then ended up in Hollywood where I was hired to dance at the Sahara in Las Vegas. After almost a year there while I lost about twenty pounds, the entire line was let go. The word spread that the famous Donn Arden was in town and was auditioning for a replacement for his show at the Desert Inn. I got an appointment, and with Donn sitting in the audience, Jerry Jackson (now the creator/director of the *Folies Bergere*) gave me my audition. I was hired, but not for the Desert Inn. Donn asked if I would move to Hollywood where he was putting in a show at the Moulin Rouge that would run for a year! He said I'd have to do the audition, a long one, in L.A. for the job, but he was sure I would pass. He gave me a phone number to call when I got there.

The audition in Hollywood lasted for three days, from starting line-up ankles together, to very difficult jazz combinations the third day. At the end of that third day, about thirty girls were left, and we were again asked to line-up across the stage. The selected dancers were called forward by name, down four steps to the judges table, to sign contracts. When they called out Betty Bunch, I floated on a pink cloud to the table. Donn introduced his company manager, his two chore-ographers, his personal secretary, and his principal dancer.

Standing there in front of them, Donn said, "Betty, we have all agreed that you have the best legs we've ever seen."

I managed a, "Thank you," then shot right up to the three-story ceiling and floated gently down again, never to be the same.

I signed the one-year contract, stayed almost four years, even got to do movies in the daytime. I was in Heaven. God does answer little girls' prayers, even those from the sticks of nowhere.

Chapter 8

Plastic Surgery

I'm sure it comes as no surprise to you that entertainers are major users of plastic surgery options. I've talked before about silicone implants on the showgirls, dancers and cocktail waitresses who work on the Strip, usually gotten because they were told they couldn't work otherwise. Film actresses rely on surgery to keep them working or get them started in the first place. The current fad is getting Botox, which means you can't frown or lift your eyebrows, a bad thing for an actress. Worse than that, I think, is getting lip injections so as to be as fat-lipped as Angelina Jolie. It looks ridiculous on most women. I wouldn't think of using either of those procedures.

In 1962 in Hollywood, I was taking acting lessons from a famous teacher and had been cast as the lead in a play to be done at the Toluca Lake Playhouse. I even had a manager and a SAG card from doing *77 Sunset Strip*. The future looked bright. George Sidney, the legendary director, cast me as a Ziegfeld showgirl in *The Helen Morgan Story*, a tiny role, but wow, he picked me! I also did a role in *I'm Dickens, He's Fenster*.

Then one morning, I looked in the mirror and saw a small pea-sized lump in my cheek. I was cavalier about it until my manager noticed it and said, "Betty, you've got to have that removed. It will show on film."

He then suggested I see a plastic surgeon so I wouldn't have a scar. I did see one, supposedly a great one. He charged me $50 to consult (it's usually free), then said he wanted $5,000 more to remove it and couldn't promise not to leave a scar. This was a fortune then, impossible for me even to consider. Now that I have years of experience, what he should have said was, "Dear, have any doctor cut it out, take three stitches, hide the scar with makeup until it fades, which it will, sooner than you think." But he didn't say that.

So, I used the gypsy phone tree until I found out about a cut-rate plastic surgeon in Long Beach, who was probably the first doctor to operate in his own office surgical suite. He did it by injecting Novocain and morphine, with one nurse. He was also famous (notorious) for doing his own nose job with a mirror, and of course, the Novocain and morphine. Three years later he killed himself, poor man.

At my appointment, he said, "Oh, the cyst in your cheek is nothing, we can fix that in ten minutes, but what else are we going to do? What do you mean, nothing? Isn't there anything you don't like about your face?" I admitted I didn't like my chin.

"That's it! We'll put a cleft in your chin and you'll look just like Ava Gardner!

The girlfriend I'd brought with me agreed that would be terrific, and it was only $300. Fool that I am, I went for it, paid for my foolishness with years of trouble with the scar under my chin, and the cleft filled in after about three years. He was a great salesman, and I'm gullible.

I had to take a break just now, as writing about this makes me sick. Twenty or so years later, the skin behind the scar fell and really looked awful and glaringly unnatural, so I traded a Phoenix surgeon $3,000 worth of 18-karat gold from one of my husband Joel's failed businesses (jewelry) for a full face-lift. I did look better, and I got three acting jobs in a row. But, nothing lasts in plastic surgery, so in fifteen years my redhead in the Mojave skin was pretty saggy again. I had three more face-lifts done, none well done except the only one I recommend, the Life Style Lift. I even had the Thread Lift, and Dr. Sheldon fixed the "under the chin" scar at last, the only plastic doc that ever did. He is a marvelous doctor, it was his greedy wife who got him sent to jail. However, one thread got infected (she forgot to give me the antibiotic pills) and finally had to be removed by the handsome Dr. Trowel after he did my Life Style Lift. Dr. Trowel is wonderful.

The Life Style Lift is the only one that actually makes you look younger. Otherwise, you may look better, but not younger. Isn't it sad that people hooked on Hollywood hopes and dreams need to go through all that? Actually, my personal anxiety about how I look started in Texas with the inordinate emphasis on how a girl looks. Even little girls' looks are pointed out.

I once asked my aunt if I was going to be pretty when I grew up. She answered, after a long pause (ouch), "You're pretty when you smile, Betty." So, I've spent the last seventy years grinning like an idiot — and getting plastic surgery so I could maybe be good enough.

What I really needed to do was stick to a diet, as fat is the big no-no in film. Sigh. George Sidney thought I was OK to play a Ziegfeld girl, and Donn Arden hired me to walk through the stage door at the Moulin Rouge through the arch that said, "Through these portals walk the most beautiful girls in the world." That was a nightly thrill. I wish I could have believed it in my heart.

Everything would be great if I could just convince myself that any of this is important. Truly, it isn't. I've known several women who were plain or unattractive but who made an effort with makeup and hair and gave the impression they were raving beauties. But in my defense, working in film is different in that a certain symmetry is required, even in extreme characters such as Marjorie Main or Dorothy Hamilton (the wicked witch of the East). Otherwise it looks like something is out of focus. All my plastic work was in hopes of correcting an imbalance in my face. One of those unnamed surgeons actually left me with the left side of my face a half-inch lower than the right. No kidding.

I'd love to have been Marjorie Main. My biggest success as an actress was playing Aunt Eller in a huge production of *Oklahoma!* in Tulsa. It was the biggest tourist attraction in the state, distinguished by the use of live animals, horses, and donkeys. Curly entered from a meadow a block away on a white stallion, the chorus entered on real wagons pulled by horses, four-ups. It was terrific. I was the Equity guest artist for three summers, 250 performances. Plastic surgery, looks in general, had nothing to do with it. I signed about thirty autographs per night and received many accolades.

As
Aunt Eller

Chapter 9

Donn Arden

*P*roducer Donn Arden was what gay people call an Evil Queen. He was imperial in manner and expectation, caustic, sadistic, and supremely confident. We were all terrified of him but would also do almost anything to gain his approval. He still appears in my anxiety dreams even after all these years.

Mother asked me once what on earth he could say to us, his performers, to make us so afraid of him. At the next audition (we had to re-audition every year for the next new show) I resolved to memorize his remarks made during his inspection of the lined up, ankles together, dancers. Hands clasped behind his back like Napoleon he slowly walked down the line looking us up and down as if we were steaks and he was throwing a barbecue. If he stopped in front of someone, we all held our breath. Here are the remarks I memorized:

In front of two girls who arrived together, obviously friends: "Get off my stage. I don't hire pigs."

Next stop: "Get a nose job and come back next year."

Next stop: "Well now, Jewel. How long have you worked for me? Four or five years? You've been an excellent employee. But, kid, you're lookin' old. It's time to go open that dance studio."

"Could I have just one more year? Please, Donn!"

"Sorry Kid, you're out."

The first three girls sobbed on the way off stage. Jewel held her head high until she was off stage, then collapsed, hands over face.

The really awful thing about Donn's remarks was that they were truthful in the most part. The two girls were overweight. The other girl did need a nose job, so maybe Donn did her a favor to tell her so. Jewel was starting to look older than the rest of us. But Donn never softened the truth or spoke in private as kinder people do.

Former Las Vegas Mayor Oscar Goodman likes to say that the dancers and showgirls working on the Strip made Las Vegas what it is today. The tall, long-legged, pretty girl in the plumbed headdress became the iconic symbol, recognized all over the world, of Las Vegas. And guess who created that showgirl? Donn Arden, that's who. I'll get a lot of arguments about this and yes, my friend Lisa Metford appeared at the Riviera in 1957 in the nude, but she was forbidden to move, not even a little bit, so she could be called "living art " and not be arrested. Monty Proser's show to open the Tropicana had gorgeous showgirls, but they were not nude. Later, they became nudes for the *Folies Bergere*, but didn't do anything but walk. Minsky's at the Dunes had nudes alright but they were doing a burlesque show, a far cry from Donn's elegant small breasted dancing showgirl ladies. Barry Ashton's nudes at the Silver Slipper couldn't wear tall feather headdresses because the ceiling was too low.

Donn was the conceiver, director, and choreographer for shows at the Desert Inn (*Hello America*), the Stardust (*Lido De Paris*), and the old MGM now Bally's (*Jubilee!*), which is still running after thirty years. He also had big shows running in Reno (Sparks actually) and Hollywood, where I worked for him.

Our direct daily boss was Ffolliott LeCoque, known to most as Fluff.

I adore Fluff. Some people don't. She was tough and wouldn't tolerate tardiness, sloppiness or any form of lack of discipline. On the first day of rehearsal, Fluff made a little speech explaining that the third time we were late we would be fired. No excuses. She suggested we keep a $20 bill tucked away in our billfolds, so we could always take a taxi if our car wouldn't start or if we had a flat tire. She also pointed out that the theater had a doorman, Bert, whose entire job was to look at the big clock on the wall and write down the exact time to the minute that each of us arrived. I loved hearing him say, "Good Evening Miss Bunch" every night.

Donn Arden had an earned reputation for sarcasm, meanness and cruelty unparalleled in the entertainment industry. Others came close, but he was the champ. Fluff was the only person who could "handle" him at all, and she too knew to get away from him when he was drunk.

One of the stories told about Donn and Fluff happened on the first day of auditions for *Jubilee!* back in 1980. Donn had called Fluff back to work after a hiatus of two to three years when he hadn't seen her as she was running his other shows in other towns like Paris. She was center stage with a multitude of dancers in the house waiting to start when Donn strode over to her and said in his usual loud snotty voice, "Well Fluff. You've aged."

She replied softly, "Haven't we all?"

Only one other person, to my knowledge, ever bested Donn. Her name was Ginny Saturday. (Isn't that a great name!) She was a cute blond whose persona was that of a bored house cat. Nothing fazed her. We were in rehearsal in Hollywood in 1958.

I was sitting in the house with the other tall dancers while Donn was arranging the short dancers on stage, including Ginny, for an elaborate finale. He placed Ginny very high up on the top level in a niche by herself and was continuing to place others, a tedious process. Suddenly we noticed Ginny, waiting for this nonsense to be over, inspecting her manicure and, mouth wide open, chewing a large piece of gum.

We braced for impact. Donn hated chewing gum along with blue or green eyeshadow and spit curls, all absolute no-nos. He saw these things as cheap which he hated. Here came the tantrum.

"GINNY SATURDAY! Get down here!"

There was silence as Ginny descended the stairs and levels down to center stage. Donn stood there grimly with his arms folded over his chest and chin thrust out in a manner that suggested he was restraining himself from hitting something. As usual, he used his right forearm to wave around in circles, occasionally stopping palm up and jabbing to emphasize a point. "How dare you chew gum on my stage!" He yelled. Ginny stood placidly in front of him. "You look like a cow chewing your cud! Get rid of that gum immediately!"

Ginny, deadpan, removed the wad from her mouth and put it into Donn's open palm. Everybody froze. Somebody couldn't hold it and giggled. Wonder of wonders, Donn couldn't hold it either, actually laughed and managed a "well all right then" and "don't ever do that again" before he exited to find a Kleenex.

The first year I worked for Donn, 1957, I was the victim of one of his famous tantrums. It was dress rehearsal, day before opening, a tense time. We did the show, no stops, then changed into our rehearsal clothes to clear up some fine points. Later I was told that Donn sat at the bar in the Moulin Rouge lobby and drank twenty-three martinis according to the bartenders count while we did the show. He'd been there all afternoon.

Gloria, a beautiful strawberry blond and Donn's secretary for twenty-two years was with him. He fired her, then stomped raving down the center aisle to the stage where a lone hapless dancer stood, me.

Everybody else had run off stage or rolled up in the curtains or crawled on the floor behind the scenery. I'd been told, but didn't realize how critical it was to get out of sight if Donn was drunk.

Bleary eyed he yelled, "BETTY BUNCH! I am so disappointed in you. I thought you were going to be outstanding, but you're BLAH. You're boring. Can't you do something to your hair, or your makeup or something so as not to bore me to death? You're just Blah. You're a nothing." I stood there like a deer caught in the headlights, silent and stunned.

Donn then called a run through of a certain number. I went to my entrance place, but couldn't get my breath and found my legs wouldn't stop wobbling. We started and stopped for corrections several times.

Bonnie, one of Donn's dance assistants, came over to me and corrected a step that I was actually doing correctly and said, "Can't you do anything right?" I knew everybody hated Bonnie but didn't know why until then. My lowest contempt is reserved for people who step on someone who's already down. When that terrible night was finally over, two of my friends followed me to the parking lot to say, "Donn was just drunk. That's the way he is. Your only mistake was not running off stage."

I cried myself to sleep, got through morning with gritted teeth. It was opening night. I somehow got to the theater by 6:30 p.m. to do my makeup. Only tears kept running down my cheeks ruining my pancake. I couldn't hold the eye-brow pencil, hands shaking too hard to hold anything. My lifelong dream was in shards around my Judas feet. I was gasping for breath between sobs, struggling into my tights and opening number shoes.

Suddenly Fluff was standing next to me, patting my shoulder, and stroking my hair. She pulled up a chair next to mine and started talking softly and steadily, saying, "You'll be alright, you're going to be fine." She continued as she fixed my eyebrows, applied lipstick, and blotted my cheeks with Kleenex. She helped me brush my hair back into a chignon, fixed my eyeliner, all the while whispering gently and confidently, her face close to mine, "You're fine, you're OK, you'll be good, you can do this." I have no idea who alerted her that one of her dancers wasn't going to make it, and remember, it was her opening night, too, and she was the soloist, principal performer, throughout the show with many responsibilities. Yet she took the time to calmly talk me down from hysteria. I did get through the show but barely.

The next night, Donn was talking to a group when I had no choice but to walk by. He looked directly at me and said, "Well I'm sorry Betty, but I knew you could do better."

I had been told that he never apologizes. The next year I became aware, because of various things that I was actually one of his favorites. He made me the lead-out girl and center-pedestal girl and other little signs dear to the hearts of chorus girls. Donn Arden dancers are a special club. We know we are the best. But it took me a long time to get that.

I have of course thanked Fluff, but I don't think she realizes she actually saved my life. If I hadn't done that opening night and so had been fired, I would have killed myself. I really think so. When the Stardust closed there was a huge reunion of Donn Arden performers. Fluff had a line leading up to her table at least twenty people long all night, waiting to pay homage to our sovereign dancer. I am not her only loving and grateful subject.

Fluff is eighty-something now. When Donn died, he left Fluff a large percentage of the show as he well should have. She's at work every night, running that show, still as beautiful as ever, setting other young dancers on the right path to accomplishment.

Chapter 10

Leo

*P*sychiatrists, philosophers, my rabbi and my minister, big sister, best friends and neighbors, book after book, all counsel me as a senior divorcée not to live in the past, not to dwell on yesterdays, but to go forward with a song in my heart and a skip in my step, bravely clicheing on down the road and refusing to think about negative elements like ex-husbands, grown-and-gone sons, dead lovers of old, missed chances, new lines in my face, or worse, of Coleridge's *Ancient Mariner*, "Alone, alone, all, all alone, alone on the wide, wide sea." No, no, I shouldn't think of all that. Nor will I "heavily from woe to woe tell 'ore, the sad account of 'fore bemoaned moan, which I new pay, as if not paid before." (Shakespeare.)

Alas, I am defeated by KJUL, the oldies music station. Normally I listen exclusively to KNPR, the classical and news station, but once in a blue moon, I turn to oldies. Driving down Sahara Avenue recently, up came Dean Martin singing, *That's Amoré*, reminding me of what a hunk he was.

I was dancing at the Moulin Rouge in Hollywood when Martin and Lewis played one of their very last engagements together, and was still there the next year when each of them performed alone for the first time. Lots of press attention and lots of "buzz" ensued. I always got into the finale costume early and sneaked down to a door with a window in the hall where I could peak at the star acts on stage.

Dean's opening line was to make a fist, press it to his diaphragm, and dead-pan, "I've got enough gas to get to Pittsburgh."

When Jerry Lewis' act came in, twelve of us were chosen and taught how to mimic Jerry, jumping up and down pigeon-toed, and yelling "Hey Lady!" wearing sequined jumpsuits. It was fun. We also jumped onto a turntable going three miles per hour. Easy.

Back at the oldies radio, Sammy Davis Jr. can often be heard singing "The Candy Man." Sammy chose six of us to tap dance with him in his act. He was great fun, laughing and kidding around in rehearsal. Closing night he invited all of us to his house above the Sunset Strip for a great party with catered food and open bar.

Sammy said the house once belonged to Judy Garland. The guest bath was all black mirrors and black ceramic fixtures, the first I'd ever seen, and beautiful. I was still married so I hung-out with Sammy's bodyguard, Big John, who always found a corner from which he could see everything and not be surprised by anything. He was a kind and gentle giant to me, and I was protected from flirts and drunks. I enjoyed his company. Sammy's recording of "Mr. Bojangles" makes me cry, worse today than it did then. Sammy was probably the most talented person on earth.

Inevitably on KJUL, Sinatra sings. That day driving down Sahara, he sang "I've Got the World on A String". In 1964, another dancer and I were sitting in the Desert Inn Lounge between shows, working as Durante Girls in the Crystal Room, when Sonny King strolled by with Frank Sinatra. Spotting Shirley and me, Sonny came over and introduced us to Frank, who kissed my hand. I nearly died.

Sonny was marvelous like that, always the Prince of Society, loved by everybody. The Sonny King Trio starred in lounges all over town before he joined Durante. Sonny had a beautiful high tenor completely incongruous with his muscled weightlifter's body.

Sonny had perfect manners. He was working in Durante's act, too, in a very important way: Not only did he sing, he kept Durante in place. Jimmy Durante had been doing his act for sixty or so years and sometimes he'd forget where he was in the act. (Have I done *Inka Dinka Do* yet?) Sonny was always right there to whisper what was next.

Later that year, I kinda, well sorta, had dinner with Mr. Sinatra. One night, about 2 a.m., I called my pal Susie, to say my hotel was boring that night, what was going on at her hotel, the Sands. She said, "Get right over here. We're all in the coffee shop having Chinese food with Frank." I was there in five minutes.

A little aside here: there were no cell phones in those days. We all found each other by paging by name. We'd call the main number and request a page for Susie Smith. Boy do I miss that. I suppose the operators would still do it, but there's no hope a person could hear in the huge spaces and loud music of today. Back then pages were heard all over the hotel. I know minor entertainers who paged themselves, so everyone would know they were in the hotel.

So, I paged Susie, and she met me at the door and walked me back to the coffee shop. She waved at Frank to see if bringing me in was OK. He was sitting twenty or so feet away surrounded with friends.

Frank gave me a big "come on in" wave, added a finger circle "A-OK" to Susie, and I was in! The rule was, if your table touched another table which touched another table, which touched Frank's table, you were Frank's guest. The waiters were very careful to move the tables accordingly.

The Sands had great Chinese food, so big platters of food were being passed from table to table, everybody was eating and anything you wanted to drink was on Frank's bill, too. We had a wonderful time, lots of lobster. He was a very generous man.

However, later on he dated Susie. She offended him in some way, and she told me he had her fired.

Let me state for the record that members of the Rat Pack were consummate professional performers, they were never late, they knew the material backwards, and they always treated fellow performers with great courtesy and behaved as perfect gentlemen.

One of my fondest memories from the Dean, Frank and Sammy era, occurred while doing *The Dean Martin Shower of Stars* show at CBS in Hollywood. Being hired for the show was a very big deal at the time. In rehearsal, dancers work very hard, out on the floor, dancing full out for fifty minutes, then taking a ten minute break (union rules) to rest, smoke, get coffee, whatever.

On our first break, Dean arrived with his usual entourage of gofers, assistants, writers and five or six men who were always with him as buffers. On our next break, I headed for the coffee station. One of Dean's gofers was in line next to me, we exchanged pleasantries, he said his name was Leo. He was very nice, silver-haired, well dressed and we just continued our conversation as I returned to my place where I'd settled in with my coat and big bag for holding dancers gear, coffee in hand. Leo politely asked if he could join me, I said certainly, please do. I have manners too. So we chatted about this and that for the next three days of rehearsal. He was charming and easy to talk to, not always the case with me back then. Leo always had my coffee already there for the breaks, also brought Danish and cigarettes for me occasionally. We seemed to have several interests in common. One of the other girls kidded me with, "Wish I had my own gofer!"

I said at one point, "I take it you work for Dean, is that right?"

He said, "Oh absolutely."

"What is your job?" I asked.

"I carry the bottle," he said.

Duh on my part. The fifth day of rehearsal was dress and we didn't go to the audience area in costume, I didn't see Leo and realized I missed him. Then it was tape day, two shows filmed back to back, so if anything went drastically wrong, they could edit with the second show.

After the show, saying goodbye to everyone, dressers, makeup people, I looked around for Leo. Finally, I asked one of the assistant directors if he'd seen Leo around, I wanted to say goodbye.

"Who?" he asked.

"Leo, Dean's gofer," I responded.

The assistant director stopped what he was doing for a minute and said, "Do you by any chance mean Leo Durocher, who's been sitting with you all week and who is vice-president of CBS and the legendary manager of the Brooklyn Dodgers? That Leo?"

You know pretty is only skin deep, but dumb goes clear to the bone. I could have happily spent the rest of my life with that man.

Chapter 11

More Donn and Fluff

Las Vegas is loaded with ex-Donn Arden performers. Loretta St. John, who was in *Once Upon A Mattress* with me in 1970 at the Desert Inn, and is a fabulous singer with a face to rival Liz Taylor's, told me that she too had been humiliated by Donn during rehearsal, and that she nearly left the business over it. Carl and Henrietta Lindstrom emailed to attest to my truth of how it was with Donn.

Henrietta said that Donn had broken her heart and Fluff had comforted her and kept her from leaving the show in Paris, just as Fluff had done for me. Carl, a fabulous baritone, and Henrietta are still in Las Vegas. Carl works as a marshal. Carl and my friend Jim Hodge were in the fifth *Lido* show in 1965.

Donn had a tremendous effect on Las Vegas far beyond the great shows he created for the Desert Inn, the MGM (now Bally's), and the Stardust. Retired Donn Arden dancers are all over town. When you see a woman five foot seven inches to five foot eleven inches tall, with excellent posture and a pretty face, you've probably spotted one. We work as cashiers, real estate agents, school teachers, ballet school owners and teachers, trophy wives, and many jobs and professions all over Las Vegas.

Dancers know from the outset that our careers will be short. Dancers are athletes; just as are football players, Olympic swimmers and skaters, and we must plan ahead for another career that doesn't depend on youth. I became a character actress, another high-paying profession (not!) Actually acting was something I had always done. I had the lead in the fifth-, seventh-, and ninth-grade plays, then the lead in the senior play at Austin High School and Austin Civic Theatre. Even a season of summer theater when I was eighteen, for very good money!

I got married again while in *Bottoms Up* which was mainly a six year acting job. After two babies, I returned to acting. I wasn't hugely successfully, but I did better than most with television roles in *Mama's Family*, *Who's the Boss*, *According to Jim*, and *Moonlighting*, and parts in the films *Starman*, *Mars Attacks!* and *Entrophy*, too many to name, all principal roles with billing, and a national commercial. But I digress.

When Donn died in 1996 about 300 dance gypsies came to the service at the Shrine of the Most Holy Redeemer Catholic Church on Reno Street. There were more tears than you might expect. Three performers got up and spoke about the positive effect Donn had on their careers/lives.

Donn's blunt observations were very valuable if you were able to listen and learn. His favorite adages, to "be a thing" and "three elephants are better than one" for instance, have remained with me. And, I'm no longer "blah."

As we left the cathedral after the service, Fluff invited all of us to the top floor at Bally's, where we found wine, coffee, hors d'oeuvres, canapés, and desserts. Fluff always did things with great taste, class, and panache. The boy dancer queens were there in force, dishing and making jokes. One suggested that the most suitable song for Donn's service would be "Ding Dong, the Witch Is Dead."

I was one of the attendees who cried over Donn's demise, not so much for Donn himself as for the passing of an entire era of my youth. And, truth to tell, I'd become very fond of Donn. He and Fluff were both larger than life, giant figures in Las Vegas history. Fluff still is. And she saved me from disaster another time, too.

Have you ever given thought to what was the worse day of your life? So far mine was a day while I was dancing at MGM Studios, working on *Bells Are Ringing* with Dean Martin and Judy Holiday all day, then dancing two shows a night at the Moulin Rouge in Hollywood. This particular day, I had my period and was catching a cold. We'd been in rehearsal for three days at the studio when Charlie O'Curren, our famous choreographer and Patti Pages' husband, suddenly said, I need some acrobatics here. Can any of you girls do a walkover?

I quickly shot my hand in the air having learned that things like that earned extra money. Trouble was, I'd not done a walkover in years. But I knew Charlie was easy and I could do a slow controlled cartwheel and possibly a front-over into a split. Vincent Minnelli was the very nice director.

If you ever watch *Bells Are Ringing* again, those are my legs waving in the air behind Dean Martin's head in the *Midas Touch* number. Charlie wanted legs to linger in the air there for a little bit, so I did a backbend, then a slow developé in place, alternating legs, and pulled a muscle over my stomach in the process. It hurt like heck!

At the lunch break I walked to the dispensary on the lot holding my side and said to the nurse, if this isn't appendicitis, could I please have an aspirin? She determined it was a pulled muscle and gave me the aspirin.

When we wrapped at the end of the eleven hour day, I drove home to Hollywood really hurting badly, but I didn't dare beg off work. One of Fluff's caveats in allowing us to double in the movies was never missing a show or slacking off while doing the show. We were under contract to Donn Arden Productions and Fluff could have said no, you can't do the movie.

Mark said he wanted the car and drove me to work. I made it through two shows, working hard and making the injury worse and worse. Then Fluff announced a rehearsal after the midnight show because something was wrong with the cancan in the San Francisco number. Oh No!

I thought I'd used my last ounce of energy, but got through that rehearsal, too. Then Fluff said, "Go get your cancan skirts."

It was two flights of stairs, ten steps each, up to our dressing room where our skirts were hung. The other girls left. Fluff sat down on stage to rest. I walked over to her and melted down to the floor myself and said, "Fluff, I can't. I just can't. I pulled a muscle today over my stomach and I'll never make the stairs."

She turned into gentle Fluff and said, "Well, just rest here on the floor, I can see you're bushed. And it's alright, don't worry."

We both rested sixty seconds before we heard the front entrance door to the Moulin Rouge clang open then close with a click-bang and loud voices and drunken laughter. And what to my wondering eyes should appear but my husband staggering into view with a friend of ours on his arm also staggering and giggling, and wearing my white fox stole.

Hubby dear yelled, "There she is. Hi, Betty. I've brought you the car keys, the car's in the side lot. Lily and I have been out on the town. Whoopee!" He walked up to the edge of the stage and disdainfully tossed me the keys. "We'll take a taxi home. Oh, you don't mind that I loaned Lily your fur stole, do you?" He didn't wait for my answer.

Speechless, I watched them stagger back up the stairs to the lobby. I could have killed him. Thank goodness my fellow dancers were still getting the can-can skirts or I would have died of embarrassment.

Fluff looked at me silently and sympathetically and said nothing. When the other dancers returned with the skirts, she said, "We'll just run it once. It's getting late and we're all tired, let's call it a day."

When I got home, Mark said, "Well, what do you want me to do? You're never available to go out. Am I supposed to just stare at the walls?"

I said, "Yes, as long as I'm working sixteen hour days with a one and-half hour commute and you're not working at all."

Mark and I didn't get a divorce for two or so more years, but when we did, he and Lily got married the next day. They have been married for forty-plus years now. She doesn't know (or doesn't care) that he is gay. That entire generation of gay men (now seventy and up) were desperate to hide their sexual orientation because it was against the law and you could get arrested and thrown in jail where they were horribly beaten and mistreated. It was the dark ages for homosexuals.

Fluff's three marriages didn't work out either. She has a taxi pick her up and drive her to work every night. She's eighty-two or eighty-four or so, looks to be in her fifties and is still so beautiful. She sees the show *Jubilee!* from different places in the theater every night to keep the performers on their toes. They all adore her. The cast and crew of *Jubilee!* presented her with a brass plaque inscribed with her name and installed in the stage floor, center front. Maybe that's better than a husband demanding supper and laundry service.

I know one of her ex-husbands, Luis, sent his daughter to Fluff to dance in *Jubilee!* and requested that she be trained for Broadway. The daughter was already a good dancer and five foot nine, but Fluff polished her dancing and got her ready for Broadway in seven or eight months and the daughter then made it into *Chicago* I think it was. She now makes the big money and has a solid career in New York. I met the daughter when we were both working in a hotshot convention show.

Fluff and Donn were both one-of-a-kind originals. And they were genuine artists. Like a bottle of fine wine, or a Picasso, or an Irving Berlin song, *Jubilee!* only gets better and better.

Just like Fluff.

Chapter 12

The Big Circus

"Workers Walk Off Job"

*W*as a headline in the *Las Vegas Review-Journal*, referring to the City Center under construction on the Las Vegas Strip and its "unsafe working conditions."

Dancers tried to do that on a movie we were doing in the fifties, *The Big Circus*, starring Victor Mature, Rhonda Fleming, Red Buttons, and Katherine Grant Crosby, none of whom I met except Katherine. I already knew her from a big class, Art Appreciation 101 at the University of Texas. She sat on the front row on the edge of her seat leaning forward showing off her cleavage, asking lots of questions, a rapt expression on her face. Chi Omega type. Of course, she later married Bing Crosby.

One of the terrific pluses about dancing at the Moulin Rouge in Hollywood was being able (a few lucky ones of us) to work on films during the day while dancing at night. It was wonderful to be healthy strong athletes, able to work fourteen or fifteen hour days doing hard dancing.

Ha. B.S.

Truth is we took uppers, really speed, prescribed by our doctors for dieting but also used to stay awake and energetic while working two jobs, plus the long commute to the studios. I lived in Toluca Lake, not too far to Paramount or Universal or Warner Brother's, but forty-five minutes through heavy traffic to Fox or MGM. I hated those pills, they give you a headache and you can't stop talking. But I digress again.

The Big Circus is kind of a cult film now, known only to circus buffs, considered I understand, reasonably authentic in its portrayal of circus life.

It was a huge set at 20th Century Fox, on the back lot, known to you youngsters as Century City. The shot we were hired for was to be under the opening credits, a giant circus parade including lots of animals, clowns, wagons, lions and tigers in gilt cages, bare-back stunt riders, unicycles, and four enormous African elephants, the biggest ones to be found. We were dancing girls in harem costumes, gold coins and all. A massive calliope led the whole thing blasting circus music.

The four elephants we were to work with had been spray-painted. One was lime green, one was fuchsia, one was lavender, and one was golden yellow. They had been trained to walk in a foursome two in front and two behind in a square formation and were right in front of the twelve of us. We were shown a simple but vigorous traveling step that could also be done in place so we could gauge our spacing.

Getting all the parade elements in place took at least two hours. A horse had to be calmed down and there was a tiger's cage that was especially difficult to maneuver into place. Finally all was ready and we heard, "Stand-by. Playback. Rolling. Speed. Action!"

The first shot went fine. We danced about twenty feet behind the four elephants, no problem. But on "cut," there seemed to be a problem with the production people, who were huddling and gesturing. Then, over to us came the assistant directors, usually four on the set. They said the shot simply wasn't long enough and they had to stretch it out two minutes at least. They decided to separate the four elephants and the twelve dancers thus: two elephants, six dancers, two more elephants, six more dancers. I was in the first group of six dancers. We worked in a diamond shaped cluster. I was the right point.

The reset took two hours again. The entire two-block long parade had to circle the enormous tent on the outside to get back to the starting place. Then all freshen up, replace balloons, get water, find the restrooms. Hairdressers, make-up artists, wardrobe assistants swarmed all over doing their jobs. Finally we heard, "Places. Take two," and the rest of the familiar cadence ending with, "Action."

We followed the two elephants, dancing along as before, but acutely aware of the two elephants who were now behind us and could be heard breathing. The two beasts were only about ten feet behind us. The dancers exchanged glances, eyebrows raised, but kept dancing of course.

Suddenly the very earth shook, we heard an elephant trumpet call and I for one, felt a distinct air current whoosh and a blur of color. A purple elephant ran past me on the outside missing my right arm by inches. The other painted elephant, the lime green one, raced by on the other side, and the two elephants came together in front of our lead dancer's nose with a loud smack that sounded like a whip crack, created by their two huge sides smacking together. The lead point dancer screamed, as did several of us. Somebody yelled, "Cut!" A huge commotion ensued as trainers rushed to their elephants.

I realized I was shaking and so were the other girls. Some of us held hands as we walked to our make-up area where our coats and purses were. We sat down, our knees betraying us, shaky voices asking each other, "Are you all right?" We were especially concerned about another Betty the point girl in front of our cluster, who had been so in danger. An assistant director came over and shouted, "OK, OK, nobody's hurt. We'll fix this. The trainers will walk with the elephants for the next take."

One of the dancers said "What do you mean 'next take?' What 'next take?'" Quickly the four ADs were all over us, pretending it was just a tiny little bobble, "Nothing to be afraid of girls. Get ready for the third shot."

None of us moved. One of the older girls said, "You don't really expect us to do that again do you?" The first AD said, "OK, OK, you want extra money is that it? I'll give you a quarter check, OK?"

Screen Actors Guild and Screen Extras Guild (now incorporated into SAG) under which dancers worked back then, were the strongest unions in the world, a result of the blatant overwork and criminal abuse common in the '20s and '30s in the movie industry. In the '50s, working conditions were better than they are now as unions have weakened.

In 1957 extras were paid $25 dollars per strict eight hour day, plus a quarter check for anything over just showing up. Dancers immediately got a quarter check if we did lifts or point work, or extra hard dancing, or worked in artificial smoke (commonly done in nightclub scenes) or got wet, or wore full-body make-up. A quarter check applied for each situation, one on top of the other.

A famous choreographer, Jack Cole, was extremely difficult to work for, just mean, so working for him got you the "Cole Rate," a quarter check. Two hours overtime was a check, the top of the third hour was golden time (double). So our dancers' checks were often at least doubled from the going rate at the time. Further, we were always treated well, spoiled and catered to like little starlets.

The ADs on *The Big Circus* offered quarter checks, then had to consult the line producer when we continued to say "No way," and finally offered double checks for one more shot. We dancers huddled together talking about the dangers and were called gold diggers until one of us, me I think, said, "You don't understand Sir. We're not talking about money; we're talking about if we're going to do it *at all*. It's dangerous you know. If an elephant steps on my foot, my dancing career is over and my heart is broken."

Of course we gave in, unlike the construction workers here on the Las Vegas strip. They threatened us with the old saw, "You'll never work in pictures again," and "You are costing us thousands per minute!"

With the money settled, we were escorted to lunch.

An aside here: I had noticed a man who didn't fit into any category on the set. He just observed and kept apart from the crew. He was very distinctive, all dressed up, dark elegant double-breasted suit, even a bowler hat. Everyone else was in extremely casual jeans or shorts. I went out of my way to speak to him, saying, "Hi. What's your job?"

He spoke in an English accent, said that he was a Ringling Bros, Barnum and Bailey advance man, and was the circus consultant for the production company. He went on to say he had run away from home and joined the circus as a teen, had now traveled all over the world with various circus companies. He asked me where I was from, I said Austin, Texas.

He said, completely dropping the English accent, "I'm from Round Rock! Small world!"

Round Rock is a tiny dusty old hamlet, a wide place in the road, twenty miles out of Austin. The tiny general store has Nehei soda pops, with a milk-cow out back. His demeanor turned decidedly feminine, and we dished like old girl friends. One of the biggest lessons I learned working in show business, is that things are seldom what they seem.

They called me back to get ready for the shot. The fear returned, the smell of the elephants was very scary, all the dancers were breathing hard. It went smoothly, with the trainers holding ominous looking hooks on long heavy poles, walking next to the poor exploited, miserable, and confused elephants. I was hard-put at the time to see much dif-ference between the elephants and the dancers. We too, were just livestock, props, controlled with hooks of a different kind. When you set out to have an exciting life, you have to take the bad with the good.

No regrets. We got a huge paycheck.

Chapter 13

South Pacific

*D*id you notice my name in the credits of *South Pacific* when it replayed on Channel 40? If you wondered if that was me, indeed it was, OK is. The great Rodgers & Hammerstein musical recently revived on Broadway to big success. Like all real pieces of art, the theme is still current and important for our society. The great movie choreographer, LeRoy Prinz and Joshua Logan, the very famous Broadway director, hired me as a nurse/dancer for the film in 1958. The reason you didn't recognize me is that it was fifty odd years, forty pounds, three hair colors, and at least two husbands ago.

I was still dancing at the Moulin Rouge in Hollywood, all the girls in the dressing room desperately wanted the job, too. But I was the only one thoughtful enough to call a theater friend in New York and ask what *South Pacific* was about. Girl next door nurses? Wow. That changed things. The custom in movie dance auditions was to be as glamorous as possible, hair up in a chignon, false eyelashes, bright red lipstick, black leotard, black net hose, black high heels.

Obviously that won't do for a girl next door, so I wore hair down and a little curly, blue and white check gingham blouse tied under the bust to show off my waist, black nets and trunks (in case we had to dance) and black ballet shoes. No lashes, pink lipstick; too sweet for words. Mr. Prinz walked down the line, and passed me up, but I kept grinning and mentally forced him to turn his head back and point to me, which meant I got the job! I was ecstatic. (A little side bar: the custom for dancers in New York was exactly the opposite, dancers dressed in old ratty dance clothes, runs in stockings, carefully looking like starving artists. We could always tell a new arrival from the East coast.)

Two weeks rehearsal was scheduled at 20th Century Fox, front gate on Pico Boulevard where it still is. We learned the "Honey Bun" number in one day, nothing to it, then settled down to play bridge, LeRoy Prinz's passion. We had two tables going, anyone that didn't want to play could read, nap, or whatever. We ran through the number first thing every morning.

Sometimes rehearsal turned exciting as the producers stopped by to ogle the gypsies and we'd run through the number for them. One day one of them brought André Previn in to introduce him to all of us. André was musical director of the film and looked not much older than some of us. He shook hands with and smiled at, each of us.

Some serious flirting ensued. One day André came by and took about half of us to a recording studio on the lot to record the song, "Honey Bun." We sang live while filming but to a playback.

An extra fun part of the day was lunch at the commissary. You never knew which huge star might show up. It's verboten to bother stars on the lot, especially at lunch when they're trying to eat like everybody else. Ray Walston, the marvelous character actor who played Stewpot always sat with us, the dancers. John Kerr, Rossano Brazzi, and Mitzi Gaynor ate lunch in their dressing rooms I assume, learning their lines, I'm sure always a serious chore for actors and the reason they are standoffish on set. Lines are often changed overnight so they can't always learn them in advance.

The character Stewpot did a funny hula during the "Honey Bun" number, wearing a horrible drag outfit. A sailor from the audience was supposed to throw a dart at him and hit him in the bum. Special effects rigged a small wood board to be attached to Ray's khaki shorts under his grass hula skirt, then attached a clear nylon fishing line to it, ran the line up into a tree where a sailor (actor) was sitting in a crotch of the tree. They attached the line to the dart, so when the sailor threw the dart, it rode the invisible line down to Stewpot's backside. A bull's eye every time! An assistant director was stationed in Ray's sight so he could cue Ray to jump and react to the dart. Special effects are so interesting!

But I'm getting ahead of myself: Shooting day was perfect, a California cloudless sunshine piece of blue heaven. The set was on the back lot of 20th Century Fox, which is now Century City, but back then it was a beautiful meadow, trees everywhere. We were called for hair and makeup very early, 6 a.m. The studio had set up tents as temporary shelters, with hair salon, makeup tents, and body makeup tents.

Head of makeup was the legendary Frank Westmore, still a very young man who had inherited the knowledge, skill, and connections from his big brother Bud Westmore, and as everybody said, was as handsome as the movie stars he made up. The makeup team, three men, came in where the twelve of us were waiting. Mr. Westmore said, "You take those four, you take those four, and I'll do these four," with which he grabbed me!

When he finished and I looked in the mirror, I realized for the first time that I was an exceptionally pretty girl. He made my beady little eyes with no eyebrows look great. I suddenly had perfect high cheekbones. I hugged him and said, "Thank you, Thank you!" It was a special moment for me.

He said, "It's just the real you, sweetheart." No wonder everybody loved Frank Westmore.

Then it was back to the wardrobe tent to dress in costume. I loved mine, white bathing suit with train and huge scarf made out of orange parachute silk, gas mask with orange silk trim for a headdress.

They also issued the first pair of pantyhose I'd ever seen with no panties showing halfway down the leg instead of the usual flesh-colored mesh-net hose. Before putting everything on, I was directed to the body make-up tent, wearing, as directed, panties and a robe, where the lady covered my arms, neck, upper back, shoulders and upper chest with pancake, the sponge wet with baby oil and water, so as not to completely dry out the skin.

I said to her, "You'd probably better cover my legs too. They are fish-belly white which probably won't totally be covered with the new sheer pantyhose."

"Oh no you don't young lady, you're not getting a quarter check out of me," she said. (If three quarters of the body is covered in make-up, the union says you get a quarter of a day's pay extra.)

"OK, but I think you should," I said.

Then it was back to wardrobe, on with the hose, suit, high heels, then over to hairdressing to put my hair up and attach the gas-mask with a million hairpins. The ADs finally called places for the *Honey Bun* number!

Hearts pounding, we all hurried up the grassy slope to the stage, about 150 feet away. Miss Gaynor was then called to the set, first time we'd seen her, as Mr. Logan started looking through the camera, checking the lights and deciding on his frames. (Incidentally, Mitzi Gaynor is currently president of our Professional Dancers Society.) We twelve were all lined up across the stage so they could see how we looked under the lights. Josh Logan started ducking his head out to look intently at us, then with a sinking feeling, I realized he was looking at me. He waved the cinematographer over, who also peered through the camera, ducked his head out looking at me and nodding, yep, that's it, girl in the white suit. Legs are glaring in the camera.

The directors all talked on the radio handsets, yelling and arm waving ensued, and two of them dashed on stage over to me, grabbed my arms and said "Run!" They pulled and half carried me on the double down the slope to the tents, into hairdressing first, more yelling and arm waving. Underlings had been warned and were at the ready, ready to pounce on me. I got a little scared. Wardrobe took charge of the gas mask (it was costume), but hairdressing had to get the pins, one hairdresser on each side, while wardrobe got the gas mask. Another wardrobe lady undid the suit zipper and pulled the suit off by the straps making me step up on a platform to facilitate the leg makeup job. Another lady got my shoes off so the pantyhose could be stripped down, so the body makeup lady could step in with her cold wet sponge.

I pride myself on being a nice person, so I had to forbear saying the obvious "I told you so." I didn't even look at her. Meanwhile, there I stood in my panties, naked in front of strangers, all women to be sure, but with males of unknown job description peeking through the curtains yelling, "Hurry! Hurry! Logan is having a fit!"

Then the entire process had to be done in reverse after they dried my leg makeup with fans. I did yell, "Do not poke my scalp with those hairpins!"

On the way running back up the slope to the set, one AD said, "Sorry, Honey, this isn't your fault."

"You're dang right it isn't!" I answered.

So one makeup lady, trying to save $7.50, (we made $25 per day plus overtime) cost several thousand or so, as I held up shooting for fifteen minutes because of her.

When the film premiered at Radio City Music Hall in New York, several drama major friends of mine from the University of Texas went to see it and were surprised to see me walk down the middle of the frame, big as life, then to see my name in the credits. It was a very big deal. Back then, dancers didn't get credits in movies like they do on Broadway, but Josh Logan was from the Broadway tradition and knew how important the gypsies were to the production. Further, he elected to reprise the *Honey Bun* number under the credits, so there I was behind my own name dancing and singing in a great big Broadway show!

Chapter 14

Charles

*L*as Vegas Dancers have a special relationship with Los Angeles. We run back and forth between the two entertainment centers with astonishing regularity.

I was hired in Hollywood to come over here, then hired here to go to Hollywood. I spent four solid years at the Moulin Rouge nightclub on the corner of Sunset and Vine, working for Donn Arden, the top of the heap for dancers. Every famous star in the business headlined there: Dean Martin, Sammy Davis Jr., Jerry Lewis, Jimmy Durante, Sophie Tucker, Liberace, George Burns, Spike Jones. I was thrilled to be working there, but my marriage was not going well and I was often unhappy.

The show kids usually went out for snacks and coffee between shows at the Moulin Rouge in Hollywood. Between the 8 p.m. and midnight show we had about forty-five minutes to an hour depending on how long the star worked. We'd throw on our jeans and run out the back door a half block and into the back door of a sleazy little restaurant on Sunset that smelled of greasy hamburgers and scorched coffee.

One rainy night nobody else wanted to go, but feeling introspective and in need of air, I went anyway, with my book. I always had a book to read. It was misty and chilly and lonesome out, as only Hollywood can be, and I was glad to be alone and not have to keep smiling, in the old lumpy leatherette bench and vinyl tablecloth booth. Nobody was there but the familiar old fellow who silently gave me coffee.

Then Charlie banged in the front door. Charlie was a tall, clean cut, more or less handsome young man who hung out around the show kids, knew us all, was always polite and well dressed. He even picked up small checks occasionally and liked to be included in our parties. I didn't know which of the boy dancers he specifically liked, actually I think he went with several of them. Things like that were not discussed openly.

"Hey Betty, where is everybody?" he asked, and I explained nobody wanted to brave the slow Tuesday night and the rain, and I asked him to join me if he liked. What else could I do, no one else was there. So we spent the forty-five minutes chatting about this and that. He knew my husband, Mark. I was always very guarded talking to gay boys about my husband, wondering if they knew. I don't remember going back and doing the midnight show, it was uneventful no doubt.

The next night that very scenario occurred again, or maybe some of the kids were next door at the pizza place, but anyway, here came Charles, only not quite his usual urbane and smiling self.

"Betty, thank God you're alone, I have to talk to you," he said. He took off his expensive raincoat and I noticed he actually had sweat on his upper lip and was breathing in an anxious manner. He ordered coffee, lit a cigarette, and glanced furtively around the little café.

"Betty, dear, I have a big problem and I'm desperately hoping you can help me. After we had that visit here last night, I went home and as I walked in the door, got a long distance phone call from my aunt, who is the executor of my parents' estate. She wanted to know how I was doing and what I was up to: did I have a current girlfriend, etc.

Well, Betty, I hope you understand, but since you and I had just had coffee and I was on the spot and pressured to think of something to say, I told her all about you and said that you were my girlfriend and sweetheart and that, yes, I was crazy about you and described you in detail: told her that you were from Texas, a University of Texas sorority girl, and that you danced at the Moulin Rouge. I even mentioned your long fingernails, always perfectly manicured, and your widow's peak. She then said that she was looking forward to meeting you and that, Oh God, she was coming out here next weekend!"

"We had no sooner hung up than the phone rang again and it was my best friend Bobby from home saying, 'you better be careful. Your aunt just now called and asked flat out if you were queer or what. Of course I pacified her as best I could, but I suspect she's going to surprise you in L.A.' Of course I told him she'd just called and he was right. But, anyway."

Charlie paused and sipped and smoked. His hands were shaking, long artistic fingers barely able to hold the thick old china cup. I felt so sad for him, for all of them

"Can you help me?" he begged. "Please, please help me. You need to understand my aunt signs the checks I receive every month from the estate. She could cut me off if she wanted to until I'm thirty, and I'd have no income, no way to live for another five years. You've got to help me, Betty dear. I know I don't have to explain everything to you…"

Well, of course, I agreed to do what I could. But what? He said, "Well, could you possibly pretend to really be my girlfriend? Could you please, please, just go out with me and my aunt and her friend Sunday night, just one night, after your early show, for dinner?"

Sunday's show schedule was different, a 2 p.m. matinee, then a 6 p.m. dinner show, almost a two hour break.

"Surely your husband would understand, or you could make some excuse, or maybe you'd let me talk to him." He looked away, couldn't meet my eyes. He knew that I knew now that he knew about Mark, all unspoken.

I said I'd need to think about it and talk to Mark, and we made arrangements to talk the next day. I told Mark the whole story when I got home. He had no objections. He understood perfectly.

So, Charlie and I met again between shows, and I insisted on learning my part (always the actress.) I asked his age, religion, education, family details, likes and dislikes, hobbies, taste, everything I could think of, and told him briefly some of my background. He said he'd made arrangements for us to have dinner at Ciro's, a very elegant, expensive and famous club I'd always wanted to see, and I began to feel enthusiastic and a little excited about an evening on the town that Mark and I couldn't afford. Mark wasn't working half the time and my salary was about it.

Charlie brought his aunt and her lady friend to see the 2 p.m. show, cocktails only, and they were waiting in the lobby for me to dress and join them. I wore my favorite cocktail dress, a demure but gorgeous black lace fitted bodice with white satin Peter Pan collar and cuffs and full white satin skirt, black satin pumps and small bag, and added short white leather gloves, of course. My dressing room pals wanted to know what was up. I said relatives were in town, Mark wasn't feeling well and had stayed home, and I dashed out front, up the dark red carpeted stairs to the spacious lobby, and found them waiting in the bar.

It went much easier than I had anticipated. The aunt was a nice matron, obviously impressed with me, and I simply ran with the part, even holding Charlie's hand walking out to the car, asking how her trip had been and how they liked the show.

It was a long elaborate meal at Ciro's with wine and appetizers. I loved it. Charlie and I danced one or two dances, cheek to cheek, and I whispered that I thought we were doing fine. Charlie whispered back that I was wonderful and that he'd never forget me and would be grateful forever, etc. I apologized profusely to the aunt for having to get back to do my dinner show and made fake plans to meet Charlie later backstage, "as usual," and did all the social niceties: "Sooo nice to meet Charlie's family, looking forward to next time!" and whispered to Charlie to really call me tomorrow after he put the aunt on her plane.

When he did so the next day, he simply thanked me again and gave a brief report on what the aunt had said about me: "Lovely, lovely girl, so perfect for you, etc." I thought that was that, I'd done my good deed for the year.

Then next Saturday night, as I was putting on makeup along with everybody else, and Bert's voice came over the loud speaker in our dressing room. "Miss Bunch, you have received a package. Miss Bunch, would you please come down to the desk."

Thinking, what on earth, I threw on my robe and ran down the stairs where Bert, our legendary doorman, all five foot two inches of him, handed me a huge white box, almost as big as he was, wrapped with wide red satin ribbon and bow. Puzzled, I ran back upstairs with it. Darlene and Shari, my best friends, came over to my dressing table, and when the other girls saw the big beautiful box, five or six more gathered around to watch me open it, asking if it was my birthday, or anniversary, or what?

I will never forget the moment I opened the tissue and pulled out a six-foot long, eighteen-inch wide, fluffy white fox fur stole. Everybody screamed and squealed, and ooed and ahhed. These girls and I knew our furs. And it had a Beverly Hills label. A small envelope contained a plain card saying, "Thanks, Charles."

Someone screamed, "Who's it from?" I gave them a Mona Lisa smile, said, "I'd rather not say" and buried the card in my purse. So that's how I got my first fur piece, and I think, a certain reputation for being, well, perhaps more than the simple straightforward ingénue I seemed to be. I was changed forever, again. That glamorous gorgeous fur made me feel like I was somebody, that I mattered, that maybe I was special, that I really was a successful professional dancer living her dream in Hollywood. I've always been grateful to Charles for that, although I never saw him again. I wore that lovely fox stole for years and years and years.

Chapter 15

Tony Martin

I transcribed this letter from me to my mother, found in Mother's things after she died in 1996.

April 7, 1960, Toluca Lake, California

Dearest Mommie:

Please excuse this paper but I'm too thrilled and excited to find my stationery! I've been hired for Tony Martin's Act!! He only uses two girls, and we're going to the Copacabana in New York City!! Everybody from the Moulin Rouge was there because the job pays the best money I've ever made, $350 a week plus travel expenses! Chris and I decided to audition together. You remember Chris, the girl who's widowed and has a daughter. The ad said that Tony Martin wanted blond bookends. Chris and I are the same height, weight, and even shoe size, so Marky did my hair blond and used the same toner Chris uses, Baby Beige. We looked like twins, almost. We don't close at the Moulin until next week, so aren't I lucky to get work so fast. We started rehearsal Monday. Tony Martin is so handsome he sort of takes my breath away. No kidding, the cat gets my tongue. He smells great, Puig from Barcelona he said. He wears beautiful expensive (I guess) clothes, Italian he said. We don't really dance much, just lots of posing and waltzing on and off. The number we learned today, *Fascination* is his biggest hit.

We only rehearse 10 a.m. to 4 p.m. or so, so we have plenty of time to get to work. Tony took us to lunch today. Poor man had to pick up the check for a party of five, Al the piano player and Hal the choreographer (who doubles as Tony's valet) go everywhere with Tony. It's expensive to be a star.

Al and Hal are both smitten with Chris. She's very flirtatious. Yesterday we went for our first costume fitting. The costumes are all three custom designed and made for us. Tony had them recut, the backside of the trunks to show "more of Betty's buns." They all laughed when I turned pink. Everything is beautifully detailed, beaded trim and embroidered lace, lots of rhinestones, no tacky sequins.

Mark is not thrilled with my going to New York for four weeks, but he's happy for me of course. We've been fighting a little ... stretching my paycheck to cover his school and everything else isn't easy. But he graduates in June. A year goes by so fast! And like I said he did a good job on my hair. We have our eyes on a salon here in Toluca Lake that might hire him.

I must go to work. I make a special effort to be early and work extra hard when doing another job in the daytime because Fluff gives her permission only if you promise not to slack off or be "tired."

All my love, from Marky, too,

Your baby, B.

And thus began maybe the most exciting two months of my life up to then, excepting perhaps doing *South Pacific*.

Chris and I were shown the town by the likes of Walter Winchell, Danny Stridella of Danny's Hideaway (who brought thirty people to opening night), Guy Marks, the comedian who opened our show, and unbelievably, the terrible tempered, reclusive Jules Podell himself, who owned the Copa and who bossed his employees like a sultan by banging his huge gold signet ring on the nearest object. The louder he banged the faster you'd better respond. He looked much like a large frog.

My birthday, May 21, just happened to fall on an important event in Mr. Podell's life: a reunion with his best friend and friend's wife from high school. It was painfully evident that the two men wanted to impress each other. Mr. Podell knew it was my birthday as Tony had a cake and champagne delivered to our dressing room from the Copa kitchen and came in person to sing "Happy Birthday" and also delivered the message that Mr. Podell wanted both of us to join him upstairs for dinner.

This was an unheard of summons and had nothing to do with my birthday. Every entertainer who ever worked the Copa knew about Jules Podell's terrifying manner, his contempt for entertainers in general, and his probable connection to the mob.

The couple he was bent on impressing was straight out of Damon Runyon's *Guys and Dolls*. Both had Brooklyn accents with "dees, dem and doze" language, with broken nose and chin scars. I didn't know how on earth the lady could lift her hand with a diamond as big as a quarter surrounded by one caret diamonds on her ring finger. She also had on real pearls, opera length, double strains, gold jeweled chains, and a huge clanking charm bracelet, pinky rings galore, peroxide blond hair and 38 double D's spilling out of her dress. Mr. Podell acted as if we were his daughters, big smile on his face. We'd been there almost three weeks and had never seen him smile.

Dinner went on and on. Another birthday cake appeared. When we left to do the midnight show, Mr. Podell insisted that we return after for coffee and brandy. He and his friend were still telling stories and hooting with glee when we returned. About 2:30 a.m. he asked to be brought a phone and called the Crosby Brothers who were appearing at the Latin Quarter, and asked them to join us at the Brasserie, a popular late night place.

When we all arrived in a parade of taxis we were suddenly joined by Walter Winchell, Guy Marks, who opened our show for Tony, and a National Enquirer editor that Guy warned us not to talk to because he'd print awful things. With Podell's party of five, three Crosbys (Gary didn't come) Walter, Guy and the newspaper man, we needed a table for twelve. We all ordered alcoholic drinks and breakfast food. Then it got to be 3:45 a.m., and someone said to Chris and me, "Oh boy, this is going to get interesting. Bars must close at 4 a.m., it's a state law. How are the waiters going to tell Jules Podell that he can't have another drink?! I heard Mr. Podell call out, "Bring us another round!"

Believe it or not, eighteen, maybe twenty, busboys, cooks, dishwashers, and waiters suddenly appeared. They stood shoulder to shoulder with their backs to us, ringing our table so no one could see us. At the same time, waiters appeared with our drinks, served in coffee cups, and also placed bottles of Scotch, vodka, etc. on the table, and the party continued.

I don't remember how this all ended. I think someone put us in a taxi, probably Walter Winchell who didn't drink.

Chapter 16

Eulogy for Innocence

*F*olks like to ask me how it was in Las Vegas when the Mafia ran the casinos. Like most old timers, I loved it, thought it was wonderful, certainly better than now. We all knew each other, and I never bought a drink, almost never bought a sandwich. I've changed a couple of names for this part of the story.

The rare "mob associated" boss I met working on the strip in the late fifties and sixties was nice, no visible horns, just hard-working men earning a living doing legally what they had done illegally in their youth and leaning over backwards to be legitimate. They were tough and you didn't cross them, but for the most part, they were like any other self-made executive. They were only identified in whispers.

Only the Flamingo had visibly uncouth "suits," greasy hair, dirty fingernails, bad grammar, potty mouths.

I was still a very innocent, no street smarts, married to a gay man, young girl when my best friend Chris and I got the job as "bookends" with Tony Martin and went to New York City to play the famous Copacabana Supper Club. Mr. Martin was a huge star, breathtaking in person, and paid extremely well. I was so excited, yet scared of I didn't know what, but totally thrilled to see New York City, and to spend time away from my husband. Chris had taken me under her sophisticated wing, and informed me that everyone at the Moulin Rouge in Hollywood, where I'd danced for over three years, knew my husband was gay and wondered when I'd find out. She kindly counseled me that it was time to face the truth, get a divorce and get on with my life if I was not happy.

Chris knew the big city well, having danced at the Latin Quarter. She called old friends and found a musician she knew who had an empty bedroom and bath close to the Copa and would love extra money, so we were fixed for the four week run. Two days before opening, we arrived, got settled, and taxied over to Tony's hotel, the Essex House, where Tony had invited us for a party in his suite our first night in New York. Al, his accompanist, and Hal, our choreographer who doubled as Tony's valet, were also there. It was fun, but Chris went back to our place early, Hal and Al disappeared, and there I was with Tony and the scant remains of a fifth of Ballentyne Scotch. Tony said he wanted to know all about me, so I told him my life story in five minutes including that I was trying to work up the courage to leave my husband and why. I was actually surprised when he made the big pass, but he didn't know that little Texas girls are born with one hollow leg and I was soberer than he thought. Saving face, he said he was going to find a rich bachelor for me while we were in New York, so if he brought a fellow around to meet me, for me not to say no. He escorted me down to the taxi stand like the perfect gentleman he is.

I've regretted saying no for these many years. Tony Martin is wonderful and beyond sexy. But he had a wife, my idol, Cyd Charesse. I was a square and stupid idiot.

Opening night was like a movie: beautiful people, Walter Winchell in person, the Crosby boys, and a famous restaurant owner who brought along a party of thirty friends as his guests. Half of these glamorous people came backstage and we met them. Tony knew them all. Several of them came back to see the show again later, then took us out to breakfast after the midnight show. Guy Marks, often joined us, sometimes Tony, too.

Guy was hilarious, we became good friends. "Oh, your red scarf matches your eyes...."

A week or so later, Tony tapped on our dressing room door and introduced his "old friend" Chet. Chet was nice looking enough, well groomed and wore an obviously expensive suit and turnout. But the most outstanding and unusual thing about him was the fabulous smell surrounding his person.

"Joy" he said, "A women's perfume, but I like it. I'll give you a bottle."

Tony said, "Betty, I promised Chet that you would have dinner with him between shows."

Chet gave me a big smile and said, "I'll meet you at the top of the stairs, OK?"

He was a little too old for me, but attractive and dancers are always hungry. And anyway, Tony had introduced him.

I dressed and joined him. I should have suspected something by the waiter's and busboy's attitudes. They were all over us, filling my water glass after one little sip, hovering behind our chairs.

I finally asked, "Chet, why all this attention?"

He gave a dismissive wave of his hand, and they all disappeared. After dinner he said he'd like to buy me a drink after the show, and that I should meet him at a certain curve in the bar. I did so, and we had a pleasant hour.

When I said it was time to go home, he said, "I'm giving a party at my hotel tomorrow night and you're invited. Will you come?"

"What's the occasion? " I asked.

"I just like to have people over, especially you, promise you'll come," he answered.

I said OK, and the next night after our shows and a backstage phone call from Chet to remind me, I took a taxi to his hotel, and called from the lobby to say, "Is the party still going on?"

Would you believe, when he opened the door to his room, he was in a robe and no one else was there? What? Would you believe we had a drink, talked, and kissed and eventually made love with me fully dressed and crying? Really. Gag.

Chet gave me a bottle of Joy, walked me to the taxi stand, prepaid the driver, and said he'd call me tomorrow. He did. He said he'd fallen in love with me, but had to go to Miami for a few days, and would call from there.

That night he sent roses backstage, called on the backstage phone to say he was in Miami and missed me.

Al was in the hall and said, "Hey Betty, you got a fellow? Who is he, tell me about him."

Al was born in New York, knew everyone and everything. I told him Tony had introduced Chet to me, Chet Black.

"Oh my God! He didn't," he said. "Not Chet Black. Has Tony lost his mind! Betty, you've got to get away from him, have nothing to do with him. He's an enforcer. The last girl he fell in love with had a husband, too, and the husband went over a cliff in his car. He wears Joy because that's his calling card, when he does someone in, the scene and the victim smell of Joy. It's a message that he did it. He's an enforcer! I don't know what Tony was thinking, but get away from him!"

Chet called from Miami again the next night to say he'd be back in New York tomorrow, and would be at the Copa after our last show, adding that I should meet him at that curve in the bar where we sat before.

I took a deep breath and said, "Oh dear. I'm afraid I have a date tomorrow after the show."

"Don't give me that crap, Betty," Chet said. "You'll meet me, little girl, or you'll be sorry." His voice had taken on a strange tone, unmistakably threatening, very frightening and serious.

"But, but..." I said.

"But nothing," he said. "Be there." Then he hung up in my ear. I didn't sleep much that night.

People we had met came almost every night to take us to breakfast after the last show, a lovely tradition in showbiz. For instance, Walter Winchell came by often. He was a night-owl and had a police radio in his car. Once he took Chris and me to a deli on Wall Street where I had a fit over Jewish sweet butter. Mr. Winchell bought me a pound to take home.

Another regular was Sammy, the restaurant owner who brought thirty people to opening night. He gave us a blanket invitation to have dinner at his steakhouse as his guests. I was especially fond of him. He was very fatherly, thoughtful, and kind. He was a tiny man. I figured he must have been a jockey. He was always dressed in a suit and had an old fashioned formal manner. Sammy was a sweetheart.

The night came. I was trapped, didn't know what to do. Then, thank God, Sammy came in the backstage door and said, "Hi Betty. Where is everybody?"

I told him Tony and Guy had gone already, Chris had a date and was gone.

He said, "Great. You and I can go to breakfast. OK?"

I found myself saying, "I'd love to!"

We went upstairs to the front of the Copa, where the doorman whistled for Sammy's limo. He helped me into the plush backseat and told the driver where to go. As we pulled away from the club, I suddenly realized the seriousness of what I had done and couldn't stop the tears running down my cheeks.

Sammy pulled a handkerchief out of his pocket and said, "Baby, what is it? Who's hurt my baby?" as he mopped my face. I spilled the beans and told him everything that Al had said about Chet, including that I was supposed to be meeting him at the bar in fifteen minutes.

Sammy leaned forward, tapped on the glass separating us from the driver and said, "Turn around. Back to the Copa." He sat back, looking very serious and said, "Don't worry. I'll take care of this."

Back inside the club, Sammy asked me to show him exactly where I was to meet Chet. We sat there, and he ordered drinks. He said, "When he sees you're with me, he'll go away."

We sipped our drinks and chatted a little. After twenty minutes or so, looking at his watch, Sammy said he'd have me taken home now, escorted me back out front to his limo, directed the driver to take me home then return to get him. He gave me a cuddle-hug and said, "Don't worry, baby, every thing's OK. No one's going to bother you."

As soon as we got to work the next evening, Al knocked on our dressing room door, came in and said, "Betty, what happened. Tell me what happened?"

I related the details to him. He sat pensively for a moment, and then said, "Yeah. That makes sense. Sammy is a lot higher up in the Mafia than Chet is."

I named one of my sons after that dear man.

Chapter 17

The Concord Hotel with Tony Martin

I think the main purpose of Christmas is to teach children that if you can decide exactly what you want, make a list and check it twice, then even in the darkest, longest night you can still believe that Santa Claus, God, or Heavenly Father, will give you what you want, providing you have worked for it and providing you totally believe.

I've personally had so many dreams come true that I do indeed believe that I will always get what I think/dream about. That idea is now called *The Secret* and is a national bestseller.

One of my best, however shallow, dreams come true had to do with clothes. I love clothes. The dream came true while working for Tony Martin in 1960. Tony was one of Las Vegas' biggest stars, usually worked at the Flamingo, then later at the Desert Inn. Our tour started at the Copacabana in New York City and was supposed to end at the Desert Inn in Las Vegas. But in between we were to play the Concord Hotel, forty or so miles from the legendary Grossinger's in upstate New York.

Chris, my friend and the other "bookend," and I flew in from Los Angeles to New York City where we were picked up by Guy Marks, the comedian who had played the Copa with us. Guy was booked at Grossinger's, so Tony asked him to drop us off at the Concord Hotel.

Hal, our choreographer also rode with us. It was a one night stand, just Saturday night, for a full week's pay. We arrived about noon Friday, checked into our room, got into rehearsal clothes and headed for the showroom

We found chaos. Tony was furious. His musical arrangements had not arrived. Tony, the consummate professional, was beside himself. His agency, The William Morris Talent Agency, sent a courier with what they had in New York, but what they had were his old arrangements. So Tony and Al were going through the act, having the musicians re-mark the music with new notations, a tedious difficult chore.

On the next break, Tony greeted us with an apology. He said our costumes were late, had just arrived and there was no wardrobe lady, so we'd have to unpack, press, and hang-up our own costumes. We said no problem. Chris and I both were sewers and I had served on several costume crews at the University of Texas in the drama depart-ment. But first we had to call a bellman to haul in the huge cartons and open them, and call housekeeping for an iron and ironing board and hangers. Lunch was out of the question, no time. Just as we got the costumes hung, Tony called a run-through of the act from the top. Chris and I discovered we had a little problem: In a nightclub, we could see each other across the floor and correlate our entrances from opposite sides, but on the big Concord Hotel stage, we had to do the entrances strictly on counts, earlier than usual along with add-ing dance-steps to cover the longer distances to our places next to Tony. Tony was in no mood to tolerate mistakes so we were anxious and nervous.

This is a little side story to my "dream" story, but I'll never forget it so have to share it.

While waiting anxiously in the wings, listening for our cue, a short, chubby fellow with the strongest Brooklyn accent I ever heard, walked up and began chatting. "Hi. I'm Buddy Hackett. What's your name?"

"Betty, but I can't talk right now; I'm listening for a cue"

"Oh. You don't want to talk to me. I'm nobody, is that it?"

"No, no, dear sir, it's just that we've had tons of trouble. Tony is in a snit, and everything is new and different and I must listen to hear what Tony is saying."

"Why?"

"Because I have a cue coming up...oh,oh....shh…"

With that, the little man walked away obviously insulted, grabbed a beautiful girl from the wings, dragged her over to me and said, "This is my wife. Isn't she gorgeous? I wasn't tryin' to pick you up, see."

I managed a quick, "Hello, nice to meet you." Over that, but just barely, I heard our cue and hastily made the entrance, rattled but there. What an insecure young man. I could have killed him. Over the years I've heard many comedians who knew him well laud Buddy Hackett as so generous, so loving. I guess we're all entitled to a bad day. Maybe he didn't have formal training and didn't know what a "cue" is.

Somehow we got through all this and broke for the day. Tony told us to go change and he'd take us to dinner in the dining room. Over diner, he informed us that the entertainment director of the Concord was famous for his generosity, that he would undoubtedly "comp" our rooms and whatever extras we charged to the room. So, said Tony, this would be a good time to call home or order a bottle of Scotch sent up to your room, or charge something in the dress shop to your room. Our eyes lit up.

"But, I don't want to be embarrassed with greedy behavior, so I'm restricting you to $300 a piece in the dress shop," he said. "I'm personally, going to the golf shop for a new set of clubs."

After dinner Chris and I went, of course, directly to the dress shop only to find it closed at 5 p.m. and didn't open until 10 a.m., the exact hour Tony had called rehearsal in the showroom. This wasn't Las Vegas! All we could do was press our noses to the shop window and plan what we needed, OK wanted.

Have you ever dreamed that you were set loose in a fabulous store but under some kind of constraint? That's exactly what happened to us lucky girls. We reminded Tony that we needed time to go to the dress shop.

"Guess you'll have to go on the lunch break," he said.

We had already figured out that we'd have to make time to run back to our room with the booty, dressing rooms are never secure. So when lunch was called we flat ran to the lovely dress store and started frantically looking through the racks. I had decided to get only really fine things rather than lots of stuff. I desperately needed a bathing suit, so found that first, didn't even try it on, just bought my size. Bathing suits were just as expensive then as they are now, relatively. I bought two outfits: both were three-piece suits. One was a white wool pencil skirt with matching sweater set, all three pieces embroidered in baby blue tiny flowers. Gorgeous! The other was practical, a beige knit skirt, matching jacket lined in silk print, matching blouse in silk print. Trust me, this was top of the line in 1960. We actually got out of breath, got done at 12:45, ran to elevator, room, elevator, showroom. We simultaneously decided to do one of our "shtick" routines, a thank-you piece. We ran up to Tony, big hugs, kisses (some air, some cheek-chin-ear, all loud) while wiggling, giggling, oooing and ahing and jumping up and down with little hand-clap applause. We were funny, and no one ever complained.

The show was terrific. Tony was a master showman, and Buddy warmed them up in great style. Tony had started introducing us by name, a thrill.

As we said our goodnights after the show, and Tony said, "Bets, I'm going to pound on your door tomorrow morning, so you won't miss breakfast again."

Guy Marks had invited us to see his late show at Grossinger's. I'm afraid I had a little too much to drink, stayed out half the night, wasn't ready for Tony's in person wake-up call so he had to wait in the hall while I threw on clothes and lipstick and went to breakfast for the famous Jewish food. Tony gleefully ordered a kippered herring for me. One look at the dead eye staring up at me did me in for the day. Black coffee sufficed. Tony hooted at me. I looked green I'm sure.

When we met Tony at the check-out desk, sure enough, there was the entertainment director, who signed our room bills with a big smile. Chris and I did the "thank you" routine for him, too.

Next, we drove to Wallingford, Connecticut, for one night at the Carousal Tent Theater, then drove back to New York for the flight home. But first, Tony needed to stop by the William Morris Agency, so he asked us to meet him there in their elegant office on the eighteenth floor of a big Manhattan office building.

We knew Tony's agent, fondly called him Buddha, so started the "thank you" shtick for him, but his phone rang.

"Sorry girls," he said. "But I must take this call."

After a hasty whispered conference, we proceeded to create more shtick. I distracted him (still on the telephone) by standing on my head in the middle of the large conference table in front of his desk, while Chris crawled under his desk to tie his shoes together. I had on a dress with a very full skirt and full cotton eyelet petticoats, but I'm pretty sure the tops of my hose and garter belt showed. Buddha laughed so hard we got scared and had to bring him water. What grand times they were.

I adored Tony Martin. Oh, the smell of him wearing Aqua Brava from Barcelona.

Tony is ninety-seven years old now, lives in New York. His Birthday is December 25th, Christmas Day. I always think of him then and wish him well. And kick myself in the rear.

With Tony Martin (left),
Chris Carter (right), and
Carrousel Tent Theater owner Ben

Chapter 18

White Ankle Strap Shoes

One of the weirdest things that ever happened to me occurred on our last day in New York after we closed at the Copacabana doing the Tony Martin Show.

Chris and I were to meet Tony at his hotel, the Essex House, to pick up our airline tickets and ride to the airport together, as part of our contract included travel expenses to be paid by Tony. At the last minute I mentioned to Tony that my mother was ill, and I really would like to go to Texas to see her in the hospital instead of going back to California with the rest of the company, meaning his valet, his conductor and Chris.

Gentleman and star that he is, he picked up the phone and had my reservations changed to Austin, Texas, then added an open ticket back to California. However, my flight was three hours later than theirs, so he suggested I taxi to his hotel with Chris as planned, then leave my luggage with the bellman at the Essex, hang out in town, and taxi out later, rather than have a boring long wait at the airport.

I felt a little bereft as I waved the company off in their cab and realized I was all alone in the big city. I told the bellman I was going for a walk to see something of the town, that I'd return in an hour or so.

Feeling like Holly Golightly herself, I set out for Fifth Avenue to window shop. I had dressed for arrival in the hot Texas summer, middle of June in my new white pique fitted and pegged skirt, soft white silk camp shirt with blue polka dots, hose and pantie-girdle as usual, and three-inch white leather ankle-strap heels, just purchased in New York, the latest style, a totally chic outfit, not perhaps entirely suitable for New York City, but perfect for Austin, Texas.

Walking in the heels was no problem. I was accustomed to dancing in heels and being twenty-six years old and in race horse condition, off I went. I was happily checking out the sky scrapers and people-watching, and thoroughly enjoying myself, when a deep male voice, directed at me, yelled, "Hey Blondie!"

I turned and saw a huge Cadillac Limousine, black and a fourth of a block long, at the curb, window rolled down. A swarthy, mustached, dark Vaselined hair, dark glasses, dark suited, big dark cigar in hand, fifty- to sixty-year-old man leaning out the window. When I turned and glanced at him, he leered and said, "Hey babe, come over here! Come over here!"

I paused, took two steps towards him, realized I didn't know him (we'd met lots of people doing the show at the Copa for three weeks) then quickly turned and head high, got away fast.

Unbelievably, the limo slowly crawled along the curb beside me! We got to a red light and the man opened his door and got one foot out on the street. I quickly turned right on another street and walked away as fast as I could. That limo followed me for blocks and blocks, the man periodically calling out the window, "Hey, babe, talk to me! Hey, babe, come over here, where you goin'." These remarks were all accompanied by vulgar lip-smacking sounds. After an interminable time, I spotted a one-way street and practically ran to it. Thinking I had escaped, I slowed down, catching my breath, and trying to think.

At the next intersection, there was the limo again and it sped to my side. I marched off, now close to panic. It had been at least fifteen minutes of stalking. I noticed other pedestrians looking at me oddly.

At last I spotted a New York City policeman on the next corner, rushed up to him in the street, and said, "Sir, I don't know what to do. This limo has followed me for several blocks and I don't know the man, and I don't want to know him!"

The policeman said, to my utter disbelief, "I can't help you lady. I've got my hands full here," blew his whistle and turned away, back to directing traffic.

I bit my lip, determined not to cry, and took off walking as fast as I could, the limo again in slow pursuit, the man laughing now.

After another long block or two, I suddenly realized a tall man had fallen into step beside me. He just silently kept pace with me for a minute or so before he said softly, "It looks like you're in a little trouble dear." One glance at him and I knew somehow that he was OK. He was forty-five or so, and something of a dandy in sport jacket and tie, wing-tip shoes and smart fedora, pocket handkerchief flared just so. He could have been a lawyer or a stockbroker.

I heaved a sigh and said, "Yes, and I don't have any idea what to do."

He said, "Well, you're all right now. He'll go away when he sees I'm with you. There's a restaurant coming up on the right. May I buy you a cup of coffee?"

"I'd love a cup of coffee, thank you," I replied.

He escorted me inside a nondescript cafe. We sat at a counter and he ordered coffee. He kindly waited for me to stop breathing hard before he asked what I was doing in New York, as I obviously was not a native. I explained I had just closed at the Copa, was a dancer, killing time before my flight to Texas, Tony Martin, etc., etc. He smiled and nodded and said, "I see, of course..."

We finished our coffee and he walked me back to within sight of the Essex House, not that far away as I had walked in a sort of circle. There was no sign of the limo anywhere.

"You'll be alright now," he said. "Go on, dear. And good luck."

I had already thanked him profusely. He watched me cross the street and head for the hotel's front door. I sat in the lobby and read magazines until time to leave for the airport.

It was hours later that I realized he had to be a plainclothes detective. Fifty years ago, and I still pray for that man's welfare, may he be blessed.

Don't wear white shoes in New York City. You might as well carry a sign that says "Hey, I'm new here and just fell off the turnip truck."

Chapter 19

$97.50

*I*n 1960, I auditioned for Dick Humphreys, choreographer, for a show produced by Louis Prima. The audition was in Hollywood, at the Moulin Rouge, I was hired, and we rehearsed a full week before we opened at the Moulin Rouge in Hollywood for a three week run before we were to go to Harrah's in Lake Tahoe. Mr. Prima was especially concerned about the success of the show because he and Keely Smith had parted, and Prima wondered if the public would still like him without her. He spent lots of money on costumes and a company of twelve dancers, ten girls, two boys.

A funny thing happened at the audition. Standing on stage with all the other twenty-five or so girls, suddenly I realized I was standing in a spotlight. I moved out of it, only to have it follow me. Finally, I got it, gave a huge wave and yelled, "Hi George!" at the light booth. George had been the light man at that room for all the years I'd worked for Donn Arden. He was a huge, strong, dear man, friend of mine.

To everybody's relief, the show was a terrific hit. We introduced The Twist in that show at Louis' suggestion. Louis Prima always wanted to perform the latest new thing so as to stay current with the public.

I remember Dick asking us, the dancers, on the first day of rehearsal, if any of us knew how to do The Twist. We didn't. We'd all heard Chubby Checkers' "Twist Again, Like We Did Last Summer" but didn't know what the dance moves were. It was so new. Dick started us on another number that fist day, but asked three or four of us to go clubbing with him that very night so we could learn how to twist and he could devise a number.

So we all went somewhere for hamburgers and then found Whiskey-a-Go-Go on the Sunset Strip, a sure-fire place to see the latest dances. Sure enough, we spotted couples doing what they said was The Twist. Seconds later, we'd figured it out, analyzed the counts, and had it down pat. Next day Dick had mapped out a plan overnight, and we had a dance number.

After the Moulin Rouge, the company went on to Lake Tahoe and did three weeks at Harrah's. That's all Louis had booked the show for, but he did have an engagement for his act Louis Prima and the Witnesses to play Ciro's, the famous supper club on the Sunset Strip in Hollywood, the week after we closed at Harrah's. Louis chose three of us to wear our Twist costumes and dance in front of the band. So, we three introduced The Twist to Beverly Hills! Ladies stopped me in the restroom to demand to be shown the step. It was fun!

Towards the end of the Ciro's run, Louis asked us one night to stick around after the last show, he wanted us to meet an executive from the Desert Inn in Las Vegas and hopefully the executive would book the full show at the DI! Since it was in our best interest, and being young and single, we were delighted to do so.

We dressed after the show and went out front and waited in a booth for Louis to bring the man around. I ran off to the ladies room and came back to find the booth empty and the girls gone. I wandered around for a minute or two then found them sitting with a handsome, suited, charming gentleman and immediately launched into a comic tirade about the girls trying to hide this attractive fellow from me. Well, he laughed and insisted on putting me next to him in the booth.

Two drinks later, I was in love. They could have been playing "I Only Have Eyes For You" in the background. The other girls disappeared after Mr. Gorgeous asked me out to supper. I drove us in my little blue Corvair. After supper at the Beverly Hills Hilton, it developed that's where he was staying.

Hey, it was the sixties, we had the pill and no diseases. I was freshly divorced and hurting. What a terrific guy. A couple of hours later, we kissed a final goodnight, and I started down the hallway, assuring him I was fine, the hotel was safe, he didn't need to walk me to the garage.

Almost to my car, I realized I didn't have a dime on me, and I had to pay to get out of the garage! So I ran back up to his room, tapped on the door and said, "I'm so sorry, I need to borrow money for the parking garage."

"Sure, just a minute," he said and handed me a bill. I thanked him and ran down the hall blowing kisses. I glanced at the now crumpled bill in the elevator, thought it was a ten. Back in my car on the way out, I actually looked at the bill ... was a hundred! I just sat there, my cheeks starting to feel hot. He thought I had charged him. He thought I was a pro-ho! Oh Lord. Oh dear. Now what?

If you are reading this, dear man, you know who you are, please call me. I want to repay you the $97.50 I owe you. The parking ticket was only $2.50. I've worried about this for forty-eight years, and I really liked you. Still do.

Chapter 20

A Family Christmas (gasp!)

A few summers ago I noticed Sam Butara and his group, formerly The Witnesses, were at The Orleans. Since I know those guys, having been on the road with Louis Prima and the Witnesses years ago. I went to hear them with a pal and waited around after the set to say hello.

None of the old Witnesses I knew were there. Sam greeted a few fans, then I said, "Hi Sam, I'm Betty Bunch, I was in Lake Tahoe and here at the Desert Inn with you and Louis."

Sam said, "Oh?"

"It was a long time ago," I said.

"Am I supposed to know you?" Sam asked.

Dear me. The man had no idea who I was or what I was talking about. It wasn't quite like that in December, 1960.

Three of us dancers rode together from L.A., where we'd played the Moulin Rouge in Hollywood up to Lake Tahoe to continue doing the Louis Prima Show for three weeks in December and one week in January at Harrah's. Carol had the newest car, so she drove, Susie and

I paying for gas, of course. We went up Highway 395 from Barstow, turning west at Menden up a steep curving two-lane road to Stateline. It was snowing really hard. Since we were late, we drove right to rehearsal in Harrah's giant showroom, and were told we were the last car allowed up the mountain. They had been in-touch with the highway patrol. We were snowed in! Nobody in, nobody out. For Christmas!

Dick Humphries, our boss and choreographer (and dear friend) gave us time to get coffee and change to rehearsal dance clothes. We discovered the incredibly spacious and well equipped Harrah's dressing room, complete with lounge chair hair-dryers, three full, tiled walk-in showers, a coffee station, beautiful floors and fresh paint. Unheard of! You could almost live there, and later on I often decamped from our grubby little cabin and spent the afternoon there. It was pleasant to relax and read, or do my hair in the shower.

After our run through on the new-to-us stage, we were taking a break when Sam strolled over to the gypsies and said "Betty?" jerking his head for me to join him. He walked me away from the group and whispered, "The Chief wants to know if you'd be his date tomorrow, Saturday night, to see Bill Cosby's closing show?"

I giggled and said, "Well, why can't he ask me himself?"

"Uh, whadda you mean, uh, you wouldn't turn him down?" Sam asked.

"No, Sam I wouldn't turn him down," I said. "I'd love to go."

So later that evening, Louie, the insecure, did ask me in person and arranged to pick me up at our little cabin-motel with fireplace, three or four blocks away. Sam drove.

I loved the Bill Cosby Show, but the biggest thrill was Lake Tahoe itself at Christmas: tiny crystal particles of snow in the air, millions of colored and twinkling lights and colorful decorations, angelic beautiful carols filling the air, pine and cedar trees and real burning wood fireplaces scenting the light breeze. It smelled like, looked like, felt like the only-in-our-dreams Christmas, postcard perfect. Anything was possible if you believed.

Harrah's has a small homey house behind the hotel where star performers may stay if they like. After we went backstage to congratulate Bill Cosby on his terrific show, we went there where the rest of the cast, Sam and the Witnesses, Dick and the rest of the dancers had already gathered. They, too, had just seen Cosby, just not in the house booth where I got to be with Louis.

A party was in high gear already. Cast parties are always great wonderful events, full of shop talk and talented people relaxing as if with family. Food and booze catered by the hotel was first class all the way. Somebody played the piano, we all sang Christmas carols. A little slow dancing started.

Being snowed in at Christmas in one of the world's most beautiful resorts is romantic in the extreme. However, I felt sad and scared, my first Christmas without my husband, rather than mellow and horny, like most of the other girls were. Oh I tried. But in a reserved manner.

Louie put the big make on me, it was his first Christmas alone, too. But I'd already decided he wasn't for me. His only small talk was to say, "That's out a' line!" with a big grin on his face.

I wasn't prepared, though, for him to take giant offense at my rebuff. I thought he'd just try again another time like other men. I did kiss him for heaven's sake, just didn't allow anything past that. Not so. Louis didn't speak or look in my direction for the entire run at Harrah's, nor indeed ever again. Touchy, touchy. We went on to the Desert Inn for four weeks, but I remained persona non grata there, too. For the rest of the Harrah's run, he sulked and pouted around me, which actually was very seldom, just the occasional backstage moment if both of us should be in the same place.

There was a bar-lounge off the casino that became the after-show hangout for us. A terrific four-piece jazz ensemble played. They always played "Satin Doll" when I walked into the room. They probably did that for the other dancers, too.

One of the Witnesses seemed to be following me around, so I was glad for him to buy me a drink. Someone introduced us to Stingers, "on and over." That's white crème de menthe and brandy on the blender with ice, then the slush poured over rocks.

Delicious. Smooth. Lethal.

Put together Stingers, Christmas, snow, lonesome young people far from home, Viola! Instant love. To cut to the chase, four dancers took up with four Witnesses. I'll change the names to protect the guilty. One of my beautiful roommates, who later married one of the Crosby boys, one other roommate and I all fell in lust.

The fourth roommate tried to stay out of our way. Of course, nobody admitted we were actually having affairs, we were just friends. The four musicians all claimed to have serious marital problems, "Practically divorced," said mine. In the lounge the evening before Christmas Eve, the four stalwarts mentioned that their families, "might be here for Christmas." Families, what families?

Late Christmas Eve afternoon here came a caravan of station wagons with children all over the place, running and shouting, "Daddy, Daddy, we're here!" We all lived next to or across the street from each other. One of the wives was pregnant out to there, another had a baby in arms, and another had teenagers. All were gorgeous women, all dolled up, looking forward to seeing their husbands.

The four of us were mortified, shocked and silently furious, keeping forced smiles on our faces as we were introduced. That night, work being the great panacea, we got through the show, silently walking home together afterwards, enjoying the fresh air and snowy streets, to our cabin. We actually made a fire, removed our makeup, and poured wine. No one said anything about our erstwhile suitors.

Christmas Day, Louis had invited all of us to Christmas Dinner at his house at 3 p.m. He was a good host, affable and charming (but still ignoring me), spending most of his time in the large kitchen stirring his sauce. Italians have pasta with their turkey and dressing. It was delicious. We sat scattered all over the living/dining room just like a normal family, balancing plates on our knees.

When one of the guilty dancers went through the back hall to the restroom, her guilty Witness ex-suitor just happened to need to make a trip there, too, resulting in a whispered, "You rat, don't try to hug me!"

Met by a, "Aw, don't be mad, baby." Counterd by a, "Stay away from me!"

"Please, sweetheart," he begged as they passed in the hall. Sigh. Disgusting.

Finally it was time to go backstage to prepare for the show. As we exited Louis', I turned and called out, "Merry Christmas to all, and to all a good night." I guess I thought I was Santa Claus there for a minute.

It was a showbiz Family Christmas all right. Mistletoe, anyone?

Chapter 21

Head 'Um Up,
Move 'Um Out

Susie, a roommate in Lake Tahoe, went to acting school in Hollywood with Clint Eastwood and was paired with him in a kissing scene entailing lots of rehearsal. They became a little more than friends. I don't think this indiscreet revelation of forty odd years ago is going to hurt anybody.

After Lake Tahoe, the Louis Prima Show was booked at the Desert Inn on the strip in Las Vegas. The Desert Inn used to be where the Wynn is now.

Susie told us one night while we were dressing for the show, that Clint had called her to say he was coming to town that weekend to the Sahara for the national fast-draw contest, and wanted to see her. Clint was making a big splash in a new hit TV show called *Rawhide* starring Eric Fleming, who was also coming to the fast-draw contest as a guest of the Sahara. Eric was single. Would Susie fix him up, so the four of us could hang out? What kind of girl would Eric like? Oh, bookish, classic music. Eric reads poetry. That would be Betty, said Susie.

When Eric unfolded out of the booth in the Sahara Lounge that Saturday afternoon, I had to step back and tilt my head way back to greet him. Both he and Clint were six-foot-four inches tall, that's six-foot-six in cowboy boots. They were both gorgeous hunks. The four of us sat there chatting casually, the boys sipping beer, for two hours, before Susie and I had to go do our show at the DI, and they had to get ready and attend a banquet for all the fast-draw contestants. It was a very big deal, press all over the place. Eric and I arranged to meet after my late show at the front entrance of the Desert Inn.

I always especially loved the Desert Inn because of its front entrance, which looked like home to me. It was made of Texas Limestone, a distinctive chalk-white rock that, when cut, revealed little prehistoric fossils: small fish, scorpions, lovely shells, all shown in perfect detail, like laboratory slides. Smartly decorated homes in Texas often had cocktail tables made of that rock, and the front entrance of the DI was lined with it.

Eric was extremely handsome as advertised. Susie told me he had actually been cast on Broadway in a role described in the script as "the handsomest man in the world." I kidded him about that, and he said he'd tell me the truth about that later.

Over drinks in the Desert Inn lounge, hidden in a corner booth, he told me the most amazing story: First, that he was actually a blue-eyed blond. The producers of the show thought the boss should be dark-haired, so the make-up people dyed his hair dark brown, and he wore brown contacts on his eyes when working. He showed me the tiny blond regrowth. Further, he served in the U.S. Air Force in World War Two as an airplane mechanic. He was, he said, on a roller working underneath an engine when the entire engine fell on his head. After they removed the engine, they just covered him with a sheet and called the morgue. Forty-five minutes later, the morgue van loaded him in and drove slowly away, several minutes passing before someone said, "Wait a minute! This guy's breathing!" He spent the next year in the hospital getting a new face. The doctors removed two ribs, one from each side, to be carved into cheekbones and eyebrows and nose. All his teeth had to be capped.

I've forgotten what else we talked about, but we were obviously kindred spirits, both of us loners who spent our time reading, unable to fit in, we thought. We were both fatherless teens, me through illness, him through divorce. It got late and we were tired. I drove him back to the Sahara, promising to come to the old domed Convention Center for the actual contest the next day, Sunday. We exchanged a sweet promissory kiss.

I was thrilled to see Eric immediately come over to rescue me from the security man guarding the entrance into the contestants' area, obviously having kept an eye out for me. The contest was over soon. I have no idea who won or any other details, I was in a haze and busily planning our wedding and what we'd name the children. Susie discreetly didn't show up. Reporters and photographers were all over, and Clint was, after all, a married man.

Paul Bringer, the character actor who played Wishbone on *Rawhide*, joined Eric and Clint and me, standing around sort of wondering what do we do next. The fellows had a problem: two hundred fans waiting for them on the other side of the ropes and the security guards. The fans were already calling out their names. Stars, just like the rest of us, get thirsty, hungry, and have to go to the bathroom.

Clint said, "Betty, this is your town, don't you know a way out of here?"

I had done modeling jobs at the Convention Center and said, "Follow me," and led the three men through an obscure passageway down to the kitchen and out to the back parking lot where I'd left my little blue Corvair.

Clint and Wishbone got in the back seat, Eric in front next to me, all three grinning ear to ear. The only way out of the parking lot was through the front gate, where the 200 fans had now gathered when they realized the stars had left the building. I stopped briefly to rehearse the guys in ducking down below the window sills, hats off, heads between their knees, all of us giggling. I had to slow down and toot at a couple of errant fans, but had no trouble scooting past the crowd around the gate and going north on Paradise to the Sahara back entrance. Eric said he would collect me as before and we'd have supper.

We sat up all night at Denny's, just south of the Dunes, drinking coffee, talking and nuzzling. I chose Denny's because it was nearly empty after 1 a.m. I still have the Denny's place mat with the few lines of poetry he wrote for me and his signature. At dawn, we walked across the street to the Flamingo where he had checked in earlier. I was in love, what can I say?

He called me from Los Angeles, came back to see me two weeks later for the weekend. By then, the Prima show had closed, and I'd gone to work at the Dunes in *Gotta Get to Vegas*. I warned Eric it was a turkey, but he said he'd come to see me and didn't care about the show.

I spoke to the maitre d' and found out that that showroom actually had a hidden area upstairs for stars so they could watch the show in peace. Eric introduced me to eggs Benedict that weekend.

But he had obligations in Hollywood, and I had a life here. Years later, I read that Eric drowned, doing his own stunt work in a white-water section of a wild river in Peru, making a film. They didn't find his body for four days.

I still talk to him once in a while. Love never dies. And when I lead an Elderhostel group somewhere, I holler, "Head' Um Up, Move' Um Out!"

And they do.

Chapter 22

The Riviera Hotel

*I*n 1963 the Riviera Hotel was the hot spot of the Strip, and I was lucky enough to be a Dick Humphreys dancer in the showroom. Shecky Greene played in the lounge to standing room only and top stars played the showroom such as George Burns, Louis Armstrong, Harry Balafonte, Rowen & Martin, and my favorite, Liberace, because he mixed the classic music I loved with pop that everybody liked.

I had worked with Liberace before, at the Moulin Rouge in Hollywood and on a television series, *Club Oasis*, so when the entertainment director mentioned that Liberace was coming in next, we dancers were happy. His show was always easy and fun to do. He had his own special finale so we didn't have to hang around and work the end of the show as we often did for other stars. Actually I loved to work with great stars such as George Burns and unlike others, didn't mind waiting.

Also, I knew my mother would be so happy to be able to say "My daughter is working with Liberace in Las Vegas!" back home in Austin. My mother was in love with Liberace as were all mid-western mothers in America. Liberace was the first TV performer to figure out that, instead of ignoring the camera as all performers were directed then, that if the performer looked directly into the lens or "eye" of the camera the performer appeared to be looking into the eyes of the home viewer! And the viewer loved that! I know of women who put on lipstick before they sat down to watch Liberace. And, he was the highest paid entertainer in Las Vegas at the time, a major, major star. It's always a thrill to work with huge success because it's so rare in show business.

When the newspapers all printed that Liberace was to get $50,000 a week at the Riviera, it was national news. According to the brilliant Joyce Moore, one of the curators in Special Collections at University of Nevada, Las Vegas, that news also set off a huge brouhaha, whatever that means, among the other hotel owners who were all said to be "the boys," meaning the mob, whatever that means. That of course, was all rumor, usually implied by gesture (putting a finger on the nose and bending the nose over) or the whispered word, "mob."

Evidently, there had previously been an informal agreement among the hotel owners that star entertainers were to be paid no more than $15,000 per week. Breaking that agreement set off a violent argument that almost became public warfare among the other owners. Really bad feelings ensued. Somehow, they managed to keep it private. Old timers know that bad things were always kept private. Murders were done out in the desert, never in Las Vegas where bad publicity was not good for business. It was a safer town back then. Old timers also like to say "they" never killed anyone that didn't need killing. Don't quote me, I'm just a chorus girl and don't know anything and I'm real dumb.

Dress rehearsal, always an especially exciting day, was highly anticipated with Liberace. We'd been rehearsing for a week, 11 a.m. to 4 p.m. with a rehearsal piano, while also doing two shows a night with the current star, as was our standard schedule. We always looked forward to hearing the music played by the full orchestra. We were all standing around the Riviera showroom (no sitting in costume!) when Lee arrived with his entourage of dressers, managers, assistants, and gofers. Liberace's friends had started calling him "Lee," I think at his request. Certainly, Walter or Walt didn't seem exactly appropriate. So Lee gave us that great grin as his helpers disappeared backstage. Then he came right over to say hello to the gypsies, vaguely recognizing some of us he'd worked with before.

"Girls, you're not going to believe my new opening act!" He said. "Wait 'till you hear her! She's not much to look at, and she wears funny clothes, but what a voice. And she's only nineteen!"

By that time the great Jack Cathcart Orchestra was tuning up in the pit. Incidentally, Jack Cathcart was Judy Garland's brother-in-law. His orchestra employed our cities finest twenty-two musicians, including the legendary Ronnie Simone, pianist extraordinaire, and the six violins Liberace always insisted upon.

As they were tuning up in the pit, Milt, our gruff stage-manager, was checking lights on stage. We heard a lone drum roll, a single spotlight tested the center curtain in "one," Milt's voice said, "Ladies and Gentlemen, presenting Barbra Streisand!" and a tall slight figure, dressed in a chic long, gray jersey gown, with a sharp New York haircut, walked on from the wings. You can imagine what it was like hearing that incredible voice for the first time. Most people remember the first time they heard that voice, just like they remember hearing that John F. Kennedy had been shot, also that year.

We were stunned. She sang "Happy Days Are Here Again" in that dramatic, plaintive arrangement and we looked at each other in amazement. We knew talent and star presence when we saw it, and here it was, a new one, right in our own Riviera Showroom.

It was a very good year indeed, except of course, for the JFK tragedy. And even that pulled our nation together in grief as nothing else had in that Vietnam Era.

I had a very interesting conversation with Marty, Barbra's manager, when I asked him how he had gotten her started. He said when he wanted a certain person, agent, producer or whatever, to hear her sing somewhere, he simply sent a limousine. He said that anybody will go anywhere if you send a limo. Even after they have said no, if you call and say the limo is waiting for you, they will get in and go. They wouldn't respond to her photo, or to his eloquent description of her talents, but the limo worked. A sad comment on the workings of the male mind. Once they heard and saw her in person, she was booked and adored.

I ran into Ronnie Simone last year and as we reminisced, he recalled that the next week after that opening, he was called in to work as Barbra's rehearsal pianist for her to learn the songs for her next engagement, a Broadway show. Must had been *I Can Get It For You Wholesale*. He said she was very nice but knew what she wanted and said so. She was also very nice, yet illusive, backstage.

Another favorite because of my interest in vaudeville, was George Burns. At his dress rehearsal, Mr. Burns said, "Girls, I have dinner every night between shows in the Hickory Room. So if your date ever doesn't show up, or you don't have anything you'd rather do, or you just want to, please join me, either for dinner or for dessert or coffee or whatever you want. Just walk on in and come over to my table anytime. Really."

So one night I actually did. Mr. Burns saw me immediately and waved me over, standing up and holding my chair next to him, introducing me to his dinner companions, I've forgotten who, and making me feel welcome and comfortable. He told marvelous stories about Gracie, life on the road, history of show business, etc. I was enthralled. Fifteen years later, I did two movies with him, small roles, but with billing, *Going in Style* and *Oh God! You Devil*. He didn't seem to remember me on the set, not that he should or would have had time to visit if he did. Stars are always under terrific pressure, dialog changes to remember and like that.

He was one of the truly greats of our business, and I'm thrilled to have been able to visit with him at the Riviera. He was doing rap back in vaudeville, as were others, but it was called patter. There's really not much new in show business. *Lysistrata* anybody?

Years later when I became a character actress, Eddie Foy III cast me as a Senior Rap Artist in *Bloopers and Practical Jokes*. For the audition in Hollywood I pulled out an old patter number I did when I was fifteen, and it got me the job working with Kidd 'N Play, the popular rap act. Everything old is new again.

Dick Martin, upper left

Chapter 23

Bittersweet

$\mathcal{M}$other especially loved Liberace, as did every other naive, sheltered, mid-western mother in the fifties and sixties. They all thought that sweet, intimate, conspiratorial wink of his was meant just for them.

So, when mother learned he was coming to the Riviera and I would be working with him, she made plans to come from Texas to see me. I had a lovely apartment right off the pool, just southeast of Sahara Avenue and Paradise Road. Her first night in town, I arranged a great, up close seat for her, comped, of course. That was easy to do, we dancers were always treated extremely well and there were only twelve of us. All we had to do was ask. She loved the show.

The next night, I suggested she play the slot machines while waiting for me to join her. She always insisted on coming to work with me. Then I'd join her between shows, show her around, and introduce her to friends. We'd eat in the coffee shop, or whatever. This went on for four or five nights before she was obviously bored with the routine.

So I asked the stage manager, Milt, if she could possibly sit on a stool backstage and watch the interesting backstage activity while waiting for me. I assured Milt that she knew not to speak to or approach Lee or any other of the entertainers backstage who were getting ready to go on. He said she could, and he put mother in a front comer where she could see out to the stage into the "one" area.

Lee, however, being the sweetheart he was, spotted a strange woman in the corner and came over to greet her during our chorus dance. She told him she was Betty's mother. He graciously said, "Oh, Betty, of course!" as if he knew which one Betty was. Actually, he may have known, it was the third show I'd worked with him. He chatted with her briefly and then made his entrance on cue.

Mother was ecstatic. When I finished dressing and came downstairs, she refused to leave until Liberace's show was over, so I stood with her and watched, always fun to do. He played "I'll See You Again" near the end. Playfully, I grabbed mother around the waist and led her in a waltz, circling the entire great, empty backstage area. Mother loved to dance. It was a very happy time. The music was so beautiful and Mother was so proud of me.

When she died in January 1996, I asked that Noel Coward's lyrics from the operetta *Bitter Sweet* be printed on the back of her memorial service program

I'll see you again
Whenever Spring breaks through again
Time may lie heavy between
But what has been
Is past forgetting
This sweet memory
Across the years
Will come to me
Though the world may go awry
In my heart will ever lie
Just the echo of a sigh
Goodbye

My Mother, Louise

Chapter 24

Tally Ho Ho Ho

In 1963, when I was young and gorgeous, movie star John Carroll came to the Riviera and approached me as I walked through the casino bar. We flirted, and he bought me a drink. Actually, his drink and mine were both comped anyway. He was a terrific actor, tall and handsome, starred in *Flying Tigers* with John Wayne, and I was so impressed. He asked me for a date then and there, "We'll go for dinner then, anywhere you want to go."

I said, "Sorry, I have a date tonight, how about tomorrow?"

"Whatta you mean you have a date? Break it. I'm a big movie star!" he said charmingly with a big smile.

"I know, but my date is a big star, too. Sorry," I said.

Then I left for my date with the Flamingo Showroom star Jack Carter.

Oh if you could have seen the look on his face! OK, OK, I was a smart ass and don't usually say mean things and I'm sorry. But it was funny and true, so I didn't resist. Oh, was he handsome.

In 1963 I was dancing at the Riviera when Shecky Green came in to play the Lounge. I met him in the coffee shop between shows when he joined a table of dancers to say hello to the ones he knew. He said to me, so you're the new girl? I told him my name, said I'd seen his show the night before, loved his act, and couldn't get over the fact that he ad libbed in iambic pentameter.

"What's that?" he asked, so I explained about the five "da das," stress on the second syllable, and recited a line from a Shakespearean sonnet as an example.

Shecky's ear is so sensitive to sounds, he had duplicated the cadence without knowing what it was exactly. I was impressed no end.

It developed that we had a mutual friend from New Orleans, Frankie Ray, a comic master of ceremonies I'd met between semesters in college.

Anyway, I fell madly in love with Shecky. We dated for the rest of his stay in the lounge and for a couple of years after that when he returned to Las Vegas. But when he left town, he forgot all about me, didn't call, didn't write, and didn't send flowers. So, I fell madly in love with Jack Carter who was the headliner at the Flamingo and was gorgeous.

A little sidebar here: if you want to see an interesting phenomenon, just loudly say, "Jack Carter" in a room full of sixties showgirls. Heads whip around, voices say, "Where? Where? Did somebody say Jack is here?!!"

All said with a big grin. Jack Carter the Broadway actor turned comedian was widely considered the world's best lover, and we all adored him. I've analyzed why just for fun: Jack actually liked women. Really. He knew every waitress, cashier, and female dealers' name, often knew their children's and pets names, too, and that included the old, the fat, and the plain. He still works I understand in Florida on the Condo Circuit, a very funny man, great comedy act (searching, needing, wanting, hoping!) Last time I ran into him in Beverly Hills he said he'd married a "civilian" and was very happy. I'm so glad, he deserves it.

But at the time, for unknown reasons, Shecky had my heart, which he abused considerably. He had kind of a mean trick. When we were sitting around the hotel with friends of his, and the occasion arose that I had to leave, Shecky would wait until I was twelve or fifteen feet away from the table, too far to come back but still within earshot, to loudly say, "I'm going to marry that girl." He did that several times. Well, I wasn't interested in marrying anybody, being very happily divorced and having a ball as a single girl, but that phrase kicked in my nesting instinct and forced me to think "what if." I'm only human. It's built into women.

He had another little deceptive habit. When we parted, he always said, "Call me. Call me first thing in the morning. Call me!"

If I did call him, he told whoever he was with, like Joe Delany the Show Biz columnist for instance, "Betty calls me all the time."

I had joined *Bottoms Up* then. Joe got on my case once at a Bottoms Up party and said to me, in front of a whole room full of entertainers, "Why do you chase Shecky? He doesn't like it."

I never called him again except once I'll tell you about in a minute.

Bottoms Up went to San Francisco under not exactly ideal conditions in 1964. Breck Wall, the boss, wasn't speaking to me because he had deceived me about our salary and wasn't paying enough for me to pay my bills since I kept my apartment in Las Vegas, then had to pay for a room in San Francisco, too. This was typical Breck, he always found a way to make it your fault, especially if it was totally his.

But I'm a happy person, so was having a great time anyway, seeing that wonderful town and dating a legislator from Napa Valley who was teaching me about wine and taking me out on his yacht in the Bay. Also, Shecky showed up one night and took me to breakfast, which made me feel OK again. Show people are big for going for breakfast after the last show at 2 a.m. I ended up driving him and his manager to the airport and returning his rental Cadillac for him, so we were still friends.

This all soothed my ego enough that I gave Breck my notice, tired of his not speaking to me and being a jerk. I was a little scared since work is work, and I had bills to pay.

Back in Las Vegas, it took me three whole days to find the best job in town, a big show for the Aladdin Hotel. Milton Prell had put together a partnership to redo, add a room tower and a casino to the old Tally Ho, an upscale motel without gaming that had gone belly up.

They hired Parker-Lee Productions to create a show for the new showroom. Steve Parker was Shirley MacLaine's husband, and Alan Lee was a well known entertainment director about town. They hired Paul Goddkin, a Hollywood choreographer who was wonderful and also a friend of Shirley's.

I'll never forget that audition. They were rehearsing at the old closed Moulin Rouge on Bonanza Road. I showed up ready to dance as fast as I could after talking to Neil, an entertainment executive I knew from Las Vegas.

When I walked in, the company was on a break. Barely inside, I spotted an old dancer friend, who yelled, "Betty, darling! How are you?"

Then there was another old dancer friend a few feet further in, who dashed over for a hug and a squeal. There were at least four more elaborately greeted old friends. They were Las Vegas' best dancers and I had worked with each of them. When I finally reached Paul Goddkin, he said, "That was the best entrance I've ever witnessed! If you can dance, you're hired."

Trouble was, the gaming board was finally really doing serious background checks on proposed partners and that part of the project wasn't going well. Not that the dancers knew anything about that.

We were in rehearsal in the huge showroom at the closed Moulin Rouge for two weeks before we moved into the new showroom at the now beautiful new Aladdin Hotel. We were supposed to open before Christmas. But the gaming board turned down a couple of partners until they had more information on them. Those partners hung around, ten to twelve of them, watching our rehearsals, taking us to lunch, waiting.

One day I had lunch with three of them and talked them into writing checks for our rehearsal pay so we wouldn't have to be let go. Paul had clued us in so we could be prepared.

We did one performance for an invited guest list on New Year's Eve 1964. After the show there was a reception. Miss MacLaine graciously met each one of us and shook hands. She wore an aqua and metallic gold sari, I was sooooo impressed. Her husband, Steve, was nice, too. The show got raves. The opening number was especially beautiful. It was a slow and stately parade of twenty-four costumes, each representing one of twenty-four countries, done to the "Triumphant March" from *Aida*.

Normally, showgirls are directed to look over the heads of the audience, but Paul directed us to do a real innovation: We were to catch the eye of an audience member, and then smile and nod in recognition, holding their gaze before moving on to another patron and doing the same thing again. It had an incredible effect. They loved it. We loved it! We got New Years Day off, and then returned to rehearsal to keep the show together.

I still giggle when I remember this little story. Alan Lee was a suited, cigar smoking, in the classic old fashioned, tough guy image of a producer, and I was afraid of him. He had the power to fire me! Or embarrass me. One day we were rehearsing on stage, when Mr. Lee came in the back of the showroom. Paul called a break and we sat down in the audience seats. To my horror, Mr. Lee walked toward me, stopping to ask Paul, which one is Betty. Then he handed me a piece of paper and said Shecky wants you to call him.

So I called Shecky, big deal, after rehearsal, we had a nice phone visit. I couldn't have a drink with him, what with rehearsal and all. He was with Kiki Page, a darling women, friend of mine. She invited me to come have dinner with them.

Next day at rehearsal, we were dancing away when Alan Lee again appeared at the back. Paul called a break and Mr. Lee strolled over to me and said, "I'm getting a little tired of being your messenger boy Miss Bunch. Jack Carter wants you to call him," and he handed me another note with a big smile. It was funny.

Mr. Prell and that group never got licensed and after eight weeks of employment, hope was gone, and we were let go. Those beautiful one-of-a-kind costumes are in moth balls somewhere. I wonder where. The show was never opened. Parker-Lee Productions must have lost a fortune

Chapter 25

My Dinner with Jim

When I was in rehearsal for the Louis Prima Show at the Moulin Rouge in Hollywood, I was dancing on stage, and I noticed a party of four men come into the showroom and sit down to watch us dance. Would you believe one of them was Jim Arness, the big star from *Gunsmoke!* What on earth?

Suddenly I was glad I was wearing my favorite green sweats top with new (no snags) black dance hose and well-cut trunks with my best dance high heels. Actually I never wore hose with runs and always looked spiffy for rehearsal. Another lesson from Donn Arden.

One of the men with Jim was Neil, the entertainment executive who later helped me get the ill-fated Parker-Lee Productions job for the Tally Ho. Neil gave me a little wave there at the Hollywood rehearsal and I waved back. On the next break, I went out to greet him, and was introduced to Jim. They had been invited to watch our rehearsal by Prima's agents, evidently to plot some booking. This is quite common in show business. Friends go see friends in rehearsal to offer support or help.

I chatted with them for a while then went up to the lobby for a little freshening. I had excused myself to go to the ladies room before rehearsal started again, and Neil followed me up to the lobby, said Jim wanted to take me to dinner, was I available? You betcha Red Ryder was I ever! I gave Neil my home phone number, and Jim called that evening. We arranged for him to pick me up after rehearsal the next evening at the back door of the Moulin Rouge. I brought a simple black dress, hose and high heels and changed into them after rehearsal.

At the appointed hour, Jim drove up at the wheel of a Cadillac sedan, but with a man in the passenger seat and three men in the back seat. Further, there was another sedan behind that one with four men. The man in the passenger seat got out, was introduced by Jim as I was assisted into the car to sit in the middle next to Jim, who briefly greeted me, and then introduced the men in the back seat by their first names.

The five men, apparently in the middle of a discussion about an upcoming show, continued their consultation. As we drove away. Jim casually asked, "Is Dino's OK with you?"

"Wonderful," I replied.

Dino's on the Sunset Strip belonged to Dean Martin and was a very "in" place and was famous for terrific Italian food. When we got there, a table for ten was waiting. Jim sat at the head of the table. He put me in the seat on his left.

When the waiter came, I spoke up right away and said I wanted a Scotch and soda then spoke again to order dinner, same as Jim was having. Those are the only words I had occasion to speak the entire evening. Well maybe, "Yes," to the bottle of red wine Jim ordered. Each of the men were vying for Jim's attention as if their jobs depended on it, which they probably did.

At last, we left to return to my car parked at the Moulin Rouge. Jim got out to escort me to my car, and the other men all piled into one car and left.

At my car, Jim gave me a lovely big hug, followed by a sweet gentle kiss, then a question, "Would you like to come home with me?"

"Yes, but not tonight," I replied.

He immediately hugged me again and said, that's all right, then put me in my car and said, "I'll call tomorrow."

He did. He called three more times, but I always had rehearsal or dress rehearsal, or opening night or a performance. And he worked all day, while I worked at night. Finally, he just gave up, and I guess so did I.

Jim, if you're reading this, you owe me a decent dinner, just you and me. I'm in the book in Las Vegas.

Chapter 26

C'est La Vie

I had another great adventure while dancing at the Riviera in 1963. I met a high-roller, introduced to me by the casino manager Ross Miller. (That's Nevada Governor Bob Miller's father for you newbies.) The high-roller, Hank, liked to take me to dinner in the Hickory Room. He came to the hotel to relax by shooting craps. He was a very high-powered international sales manager for a Fortune 500 Company. I could actually talk to him, a rare quality. He always asked what books I was reading, what films I'd seen, and what I thought about them. Also, he was a big tall guy only about fifty.

He always asked if I would like a little poke, which made me giggle.

For one special occasion Hank called ahead and asked me to accompany him to a "very important" sales meeting/dinner with "stock-holders." The guest list turned out to be all men. He introduced me to each one by name. For one he added, "He's an English professor."

"Oh. Do you grade on the curve?" I added immediately, and got a nice laugh.

Then when we were seated, perusing the menu, two of the men said they would like a certain steak, and the professor said, "Me, too. Let me not to the marriage of true minds..."

So, I added, "admit impediments. Love is not love which alters where it alteration finds."

I paused to let him add the next line, then he and I finished out the sonnet, alternating lines, all the way through fourteen lines including the couplet. I studied Shakespeare at the University of Texas. My dear high-roller was about to split his face smiling, he was so pleased with me. He told me later the meeting was a huge success thanks to me.

Within the next month or so, the Dick Humphries Dancers were informed we had a month off, that Harry Belafonte was coming in with a full show, dancers included, so we'd have three weeks off before returning for rehearsals for the next star, George Burns I think it was. This was a fabulous situation and very unusual. Usually, if we had time off, it was because we were out of work, and had to save money and look for a new job. I called my dear girlfriend and fellow bookend dancer in Burbank, and Chris said, of course, come right on over and stay with me.

I'd only been there a day when the phone rang and, of all things, it was my friend Hank, the high-roller. I asked him how he found me, he said he'd asked the casino manager Ross Miller, who called Milt the stage manager, who called Dick Humphries the choreographer, who called his vacationing dancers until he found one who knew where I was and knew Chris's phone number.

Hank asked me to have dinner with him the next night.

"Oh, are you coming to L.A.?" I asked.

"No, I want you to fly to New York, I have another sales meeting there," he answered.

His home office was in Chicago. He went on to tell me what airline, what time etc., his secretary had already inquired. He then asked if I could finance the $300 round trip ticket, mentioning that he'd reimburse me as soon as I got there. He was waiting at the bottom of the stairs on the tarmac in New York to give me a hug and then handed me four hundred dollar bills. I said no, the ticket was only $300. He said, but you'll need walking around money, you might want to buy a newspaper or something.

We taxied to the Essex House on Central Park where he had a suite on the top floor, and he had booked me a suite on another floor; a very classy fellow, which is why I liked him. His class showed in a very casual off-hand manner.

I don't remember where we had dinner, it was very fancy with violins and another table of men and I was again too, too, charming. But it was really fun.

Back at the hotel, Hank said he had to fly to London the next morning, and added, "Why don't you stay on for a few days in your suite. It would be a shame for you not to see something of the city now that you're here. I'll arrange with the manager to bill me."

So I did. What fun. I studied the newspaper and saw that a singer friend of mine from the last year at the Moulin Rouge in Hollywood, a tall blond fullback from Tulsa, with the voice of an angel, was starring on Broadway in *No Strings*. I had long adored him, as had all the women in that show. I called for a ticket, enjoyed the show, and then went backstage to see him.

He arranged to meet me the next day at the Guggenheim Museum, where we spent the afternoon. I well remember that long curving ramp, which I ran up in my four-inch heels. We stood and hugged and kissed forever in front of Roy Lichtenstein's *Alarm*. I adore that painting, and Don.

Of course I had an affair with him, don't be silly. He'd been so sweet, protective and supportive backstage at the Moulin Rouge when a certain evil queen (Larry) was in love with my gay husband, and was very mean to me and making my life miserable. Oddly, Don was often suddenly at my elbow or nearby when that queen was at his worse. Sometimes, he actually came over and put his arm around my shoulders and glared at Larry.

Most of the company thought I didn't know about my husband. I did know. I just didn't know what I wanted to do about it. I loved my Marky.

We lived incredibly glamorous lives. I feel sorry for everybody who didn't get to be a dancer and showgirl on the Las Vegas Strip in the sixties. I appreciated and savored every moment, even the rare bad ones.

The only problem is, those days are over now. C'est La Vie. That's life. But love is forever, and so are memories.

Chapter 27

Brief Liberation

The Sexual Revolution changed all our lives in multiple ways far beyond the obvious, especially language. My mother would have fainted if I ever had used the word "butt," never mind any other four-letter word. Vulgar we were not in the 1950s. Mother once was making me a tap costume and called me in to try it on. She looked left, then right, then whispered, "I have to fit the crotch." No one was there but us.

Showgirls and dancers of the early 1960s were on the razor's edge of that revolution. The revealing costumes, the flaw-hiding makeup and hair, the body-sculpting dance moves, the exciting music, all projected an image of sexuality and femininity that turned us into the iconic worldwide image that is still synonymous with Las Vegas today.

Nothing as intellectually highfalutin as all that was on my mind at the time, nor I'm sure, of my fellow performers, even though we all caught on to the world-changing significance of the pill fairly quickly.

My roommate came home from her doctor's appointment one afternoon looking elated and said she had hated that darn diaphragm ever since her husband discovered her infidelity by finding the box empty. So, hooray, now she had a little pill. I had that prescription as soon as I could get to my doctor. And dressing room chat took on a whole new and interesting element.

The general consensus was clear: We could at last act like men always had acted, if we wanted to do so. In the name of all the mistreated, long-suffering women of history since the beginning of time, damn the torpedoes, full steam ahead. We had all learned at our mother's knee that if you got pregnant, career ambitions were over, Saturday night dates were over, your freedom was over. I think women of the time could be forgiven for a tiny bit of sass. Now, men will get a little of their own back, and I'll lead the charge.

The problem here was that casino customers, gamblers, often asked one of us showgirls casually passing by to join them and bring them luck. If they won, they often said, "Here, hon, put this in your purse," and handed us a chip or two.

If one of us then subsequently fell in love over dinner and joined the gentleman in his room, was she being paid in advance for doing what came naturally? Was one not related to the other? Or were both actions done in the name of Gloria Steinem?

If the fellow continued gambling and lost his money, before or after dinner, any decent girl would have said, "Here, please, take the chips back." Or, how about if she used his chips to gamble herself, won and considered the winnings hers entirely?

Meanwhile, the palpable excitement on the Strip was daily. Every night was a huge party. We were applauded, catered to and invited everywhere. We dressed to the teeth, high heels, beaded sheaths or silk chiffon dresses, white gloves, furs, Chanel No. 5, all standard. When I first retired, the thing I missed the most was the sea of heads turning as I walked through a casino or down a sidewalk or across a street. Heady stuff for a young woman. Chubby, plain, insignificant little sister me became belle of the ball, queen of the Riviera, mistress of the Desert Inn, star of the Dunes. I owned them all. What a wonderful illusion. Delusion? Sigh.

Sometimes being synonymous with sex and Las Vegas had its extreme downside. One of the worst downsides was when one of the casino bosses attempted to turn you out, which means what you think it means. It didn't happen to all of the dancers, just ones like me who obviously liked to dress up and have a drink out front and flirt.

It had a pattern: First one of the underlings, a host perhaps, approached the girl, in this case me, and said, "I want to talk to you, Betty. One of our big bosses has a crush on you. He can't stop thinking about you. He says it's worth $100 if you will just go upstairs with him. It won't take long, ten minutes of your time, that's all. How about it?"

Home in Texas, I would have screamed, "Get away from me you SOB," but this was a good job, and I knew I had to be careful how I said no. So, I did a simple, "No, no, no. Don't be silly," and walked away giggling. I am an actress, and I can giggle on cue.

Next night, same scenario, "Really, Betty, he is just crazy about you, ten to fifteen minutes for $100?"

"So, you're telling me he doesn't want to talk or get to know one another?" I would ask. "I don't sleep with men with whom I don't have a loving, serious relationship. Wouldn't he like to chat, have a cup of coffee? No? Well, then forget it."

Next night, here we go again. But the host said, "All right, he will have a cup of coffee with you, come on. I'll introduce you." And out to the coffee shop we'd go, where I would be introduced to a black suit, silver-haired, very stiff and formal sixty-year-old man. He'd order coffee for me, then just silently look at me. Finally, I'd say, "I'm very flattered that you think I am attractive." He would nod. "Er, where are you from?" He replied New York.

Silence.

Several more lame attempts at conversation.

Finally, I lost patience, and smiling said, "Well, thanks anyway, I'm afraid what you want is out of the question. Thanks for the coffee and thanks again. Goodbye."

A very big star came to the Riviera and one member of the star's entourage was a very young man, maybe twenty-four to twenty-five, a little short, a little pudgy, but very nice and very thrilled to be in Las Vegas for the first time. I met him at dress rehearsal. Several days later, he asked me to have dinner with him in the showroom after our opening number.

He must have been pretty close to the star, because when I dressed and came downstairs after our number, he escorted me to a house booth and signed for dinner. We chatted casually between acts, and stayed after the show for coffee and dessert, and continued our conversation about our respective universities and campus activities. Then, he suggested we go hear the lounge singer, Buddy Greco, I think it was, at the Sands.

"Wonderful," I said, and we started for the front door.

In the vestibule between the casino exit and the outside doors, he paused and said, "Oh, wait a minute," (looking at his watch) "I have to make a long-distance phone call. Do you mind waiting for me? Or, come up with me if you like. It will only take a minute."

Comfortable with him now and not wanting to just stand there, I said sure and off we went to the elevator, down the hall and into his room, still chatting casually about college. In his room, he said, "Excuse me a moment," and went into the bathroom. I sat down in the only chair and waited, rather a long time, I thought, only to have the poor dear come out of the bathroom in his nice striped undershorts and black socks.

I have never been so surprised. Not a single prior hint. He just stood there until I finally said, "Oh dear, oh dear. I am afraid there has been a misunderstanding. I am so sorry." He mumbled, "You mean you don't ... er, er?" I said again, "I am so sorry. I don't know what on earth made you think ... thanks for the lovely dinner. I must go now. Goodbye." And off I went.

I left, my dignity by no means intact. His was in shreds, poor dear.

Chapter 28

Disgusting Abe

I've already talked about sitting in the coffee shop at the Dunes and getting hired on the spot as a replacement showgirl for *Gotta Get to Vegas*. After fitting the costumes that very night, learning the numbers the next afternoon, (they were very simple and I used my "swing girl" skills), and opening that night, I could finally turn my attention to learning about the hotel, like, what was good to eat in the coffee shop, where were the ladies rooms, what were the dressers names, and all the details usual in a new job. The main question on my mind was, could I be friends with the other showgirls, as I was accustomed to working with dancers, another breed entirely, or so I thought. Only three of the showgirls worked topless in the show, a frozen pose in a frame.

About the third or fourth evening I was there, between shows I dressed and went out front planning to join the dancers in the coffee shop. Two of them had become my roommates, old friends from the Louis Prima show who had an extra bedroom in their apartment and could use some help with the rent on a three bedroom place.

Walking to the coffee shop down a wide hallway, I met an astonishing sight, the likes of which I'd never seen before: A drugstore cowboy, too extreme to be real outside of Halloween, but he was. His name was Abe Schiller, he said later. He wore custom made western pants and matching shirt, both powder blue with double rows of rhinestones down the pants sides, outlining the shirt pockets and plackets and collar, matching rhinestone buttons, powder blue cowboy hat with rhinestone hat band, powder blue custom leather boots, rhinestones outlining the toes and seams. With hat and boots, he was about six-foot-six or more, a very imposing and astonishing presence.

The apparition stopped in front of me and asserted, "So. You're the new girl. What's your name? Are you hungry? Let's go to the coffee shop and I'll buy you a sandwich or whatever you want."

With that, he gripped my upper arm and forcibly marched me down the hall to the restaurant.

"I work across the street at the Flamingo, but I know all the guys over here; we're all friends," he said.

He greeted the hostess by name and headed for a vacant booth without her direction, as if he owned the place. He was a steamroller kind of person.

Seated and sipping coffee, he said, "OK, now, tell me all about yourself." If I paused for a second, he barked out a question. So I told him I was from Texas, how long I'd been out here, talked about the Moulin Rouge in Hollywood and movies I'd done. But he didn't care about all that. He wanted to know if I'd ever been married, how long, to whom, how did it end.

Finally getting in a question of my own, I asked about his clothes and he said he always dressed like that, and that he owned about twenty outfits all in different colors head to toe.

Next time I saw him he was dressed in head-to-toe vibrant pink with elaborate embroidery on the shirt and pants pockets, and the pink boots were ostrich leather. He was head of publicity and advertising at the Flamingo and saw no reason to go unnoticed. When it was time for me to go backstage for the second show, he instructed me to call him anytime for whatever I needed and gave me his card.

The very next night, there he was again (as I said, dressed in pink) to stop me in the hall.

"Listen Betty," he said. "I've got a job for you. One of my high-rollers wants to see two showgirls making love to each other before he joins in. It'll pay a lot."

I stood there in silence, jaw dropped and breathless before I managed to get out, "I beg your pardon?"

"Don't give me that innocent shit," he interjected. "You've been married. You know the score."

"Not in that direction Sir, and I wouldn't even consider it," I replied. "Absolutely not, no way, how dare you..."

He started muttering curses, and stomped off saying, "Stupid little bitch. I thought I had this all taken care of, dumb broad."

One of the showgirls walked by and asked, "What was that about Betty? Let's have a drink and get something to eat in the coffee shop."

Micky was her name, she was married to one of Freddy Bell's Bellboys. She remains in my memory as one of the most beautiful showgirls around, also very smart. She was a brunette, wore beautiful clothes, and I wanted to be just like her. She was so sophisticated, yet down to earth. Of course I told her all that Abe had said.

She was a big comfort, saying, "That comes with the territory, just laugh it off, he was just taking a shot, hoping. He'll never ask you again, relax. It's not the end of the world. He takes a shot at all the new girls."

Over a drink, she also waxed philosophical, and said that showgirls were just like nurses or secretaries, some put out, some don't. And no, all bosses don't think showgirls and dancers are available for a price. She was a very wise lady. That show closed after four weeks.

After that I never went to the Flamingo. I had heard before, but now became uncomfortably aware, that the Flamingo was notorious for having three ladies-of-the-evening — one brunette, one blond, one redhead — always in the front bar for the high rollers to choose from. It was an urban legend that turned out to be true. The casino bar used to be first thing on the left when you entered the hotel, running parallel to the Strip, with huge windows so you could see who was arriving on the long curved drive. The legend of the three hookers at the Flamingo wasn't as bad as the half-circle bar right off the casino at Caesars Palace. Frank Sinatra called it the Gonorrhea Bar.

But dancers have to go where the work is, so the time came when I was hired for a show going into the lounge at the Flamingo. Jose Antonio was in the Louis Prima show with me and was branching out as a choreographer, so he called and asked if I would do his new show booked for the Flamingo Lounge. I never turn down a friend, besides, a job is a job. But, Oh God it was a Watusi show, the latest teenage dance fad, and three shows a night.

The show had two showgirls and ten dancers. Jose had been informed by the entertainment director that he had to use those two showgirls and it was OK if they just stood on little pedestals, one on each side. They were paid by the hotel, not Jose. One of them didn't have a car and lived close to me, so ended up riding to work with me every night. She was very sweet and shy, had nothing to say. During the run of the show, one or the other or both would often be missing at show time. Jose told us the entertainment director, Mitch, had told him not to worry about that, that it was none of his business. We finally figured out they were "working girls" and would be back for the next show, that they were on display so the bosses could say, "Take your pick, blond or redhead."

Meanwhile, I still enjoyed dressing up and going out front between shows, especially seeing the current lounge show acts, like Fats Waller. And I walked by the pits, checking out the New York fashions, or maybe got a bite of supper in the coffee shop. I'm sure all this made me look mighty suspicious to the dirty-minded men who ran the casino.

One night the host in the lounge stopped me and said the casino manager, Chester Simms, had a crush on me and wanted me to go upstairs with him for $100. Well I'd been through that story back at the Riviera, so immediately said, "Absolutely not, no way."

They tried again the next night, and I said no again. The next night after the second show, they fired me. The entertainment director, Mitch DeWood, called me over to his booth in the lounge, handed me my check to date, said I didn't need to do the last show, to clear my dressing table and go.

I was furious of course, but relieved, too. I hated the Watusi. I couldn't stand Mitch DeWood, he of the greasy hair, yellow teeth, and dirty fingernails. The worst part was my friend Jose who was devastated his friend Betty was being insulted. I comforted him as best I could. Goodness knows it wasn't his fault. And goodness knows I didn't care about the job. But I'd never been fired before or since. It makes you feel sort of sick. As I drove away I yelled, "Next."

I hate to say it, but we were called Sin City back then for a reason. I worked on the Strip for fifteen years. Sometimes I think I stayed too long at the fair. No, I take that back. After the Watusi job, I went back to Bottoms Up and worked in that show for years, becoming an actress in the process.

If you really want to learn performing, try three shows per night for a couple of years. This is the only way timing can be learned. Timing can't be taught because everyone's timing is personal.

In later years, a University of Nevada, Las Vegas, professor with a doctorate in the history of gambling told me Bugsy (calling him that could get you killed) Siegel invited Abe Shiller and his wife and two young children to the Flamingo pool for a party of some kind. Bugsy got annoyed at Abe for something, and, with Abe in his bathing suit in front of his family, Bugsy pistol whipped him and forced Abe to crawl on the cement around the pool on his hands and knees until his knees were bloody. Karma?

Chapter 29

Gone With the Wynn

Once upon a time there was a restaurant made in heaven called the Sultan's Table, lovingly placed in the Dunes hotel by the gods of food, wine and music. I was working as a showgirl there in 1962 in, undoubtedly, the worst show ever to play the Las Vegas Strip — a revue called *Gotta Get to Vegas*. Usually, I worked as a dancer, but this time I had been hired as a replacement showgirl.

My favorite high-roller/bon vivant then was Mr. A. Gamblers were addressed by the first initial of their last name in those more discreet days. He was a true gourmand, often taking me to dine between shows. He had a favorite menu and it became mine.

The ambiance at the Sultan's Table started at the door, with a grand and dignified maitre d' — the famous Joachim — who led us to a choice booth in dark red leather set with upscale linen, heavy silverware and glowing candles. By then, the music was washing over the senses — music too beautiful to describe performed by twenty violins, a cello, a bass, and a grand piano all playing light classics, as well as Cole Porter, Gershwin, and Irving Berlin. When the orchestra took a break, a small dancing-waters show appeared beyond the dance floor.

All the musicians, captains, and waiters wore tuxedos. The lady guests were dressed to the nines in fur, jewels, and high heels, all coiffed, polished, and wafting the scent of Joy or Shalimar.

And then the food began. We started with an appetizer of coquilles Saint-Jacques (creamy shellfish with mushrooms topped with cheese and baked in a real 6-inch shell) presented on a folded napkin. Then our captain tossed our Green Goddess salad tableside, and assorted rolls were served warm with dewy curls of sweet butter.

With the coquilles and salad we had either a pouilly-fuisse or sometimes a fine Liebraumilch if one was suggested by the sommelier.

After a small pause while the next wine was uncorked, poured, or tasted, the Chateaubriand bouquetiere arrived — the filet perfectly charred and rare and served with béarnaise. The vegetables, carrots cut on the bias, florets of broccoli, and asparagus spears were all served with hollandaise. Mr. A always ordered both sauces with this meal. Another specialty we enjoyed was potatoes Anna, prepared crisp and brown on the side with the butter they were fried in still sizzling. The whole was washed down with a Chateau French wine, maybe even a grand cru class.

Having devoured every last morsel, I always declined dessert. But smiling gleefully, the captain brought over a pedestal of complimentary petit fours, glistening with chocolate, pink, and vanilla fondant. The pink was flavored with marzipan. The vanilla had apricot filling. With hot, rich coffee, they were irresistible. The miracle was how I managed to stagger backstage and do the midnight show.

Do I miss the Sultan's Table? Like I miss my youth, my mother, and my grown sons as babies.

How lucky we were.

Chapter 30

The Desert Inn

I stopped at a garage sale recently, found a box of compact discs and tapes, and started filtering through the box. The homeowner, a young father, asked, "What are you looking for?"

"Anything Louie Prima," I replied.

"Who's that?" he asked.

It's depressing to discover that a whole era, my era, is unknown to the general public now. I really miss those wonderful old hotels, especially the Desert Inn, where I felt so at home. I performed there three times: the Louis Prima show in 1960 in the old Cactus Room Showroom, *The Jimmy Durante Show* in 1965 in the new north-facing room and an Equity show, *Once Upon A Mattress* in 1969 in the redone lounge.

If things were ever slow or boring backstage during the *Mattress* show, one of us would announce with great seriousness, "I'm sure I saw Howard Hughes at the bar just now!"

Visitors would gasp, "Really?" Some other old hand would then insist she'd ridden in the elevator with him that afternoon. We had fun ... poor man. But I really did see him once after midnight lurking behind a large post in the casino.

I especially miss the small ballroom dance areas with live trios that nearly all the hotels had then. Working at the Desert Inn, if nothing compelling presented itself between shows, you could always go up to the Sky Room on the third floor, enjoy the view, sit at the bar, or dance if anyone was around to dance with. And oh, that great dance lounge, Top of the Dunes.

Once, sitting in the Desert Inn lounge next to the casino with my fellow dancer Shirley, somebody introduced me to Jerry Lester, the great Broadway star, dancer and comedian. He'd never been to Las Vegas and loved it. Then one of the Crosby boys, I think it was Lindsay, joined us, making a foursome. Since I didn't know those two fellows well, having just been introduced, conversation was a little strained. All four of the Crosby boys used to come backstage at the Moulin Rouge in Hollywood, but Lindsay Crosby was always a little shy. So I said, "I know what let's do, let's go to the Dunes. You might enjoy the Top of the Dunes there."

It was only a five minute taxi ride. They had a bigger band and were nearly always full, as they were that night, so it was extra festive and had a great breathtaking, glittery view of the entire strip. There are several of those views around town now.

Jerry got a table for four, and we all had drinks. The dance music was great. So I said to Jerry, "I bet you have the same problem with ballroom dancing that I do. Your partner is almost never a dancer. Further in my case, the man leads, so I have to follow him even if he can't keep time to the music. Even worse, if the band plays a jitterbug tune, they often just plant their feet and sling me out and around, expecting fancy footwork, working me to death while making them look really good. Easy for me to oblige, but tiring."

"I know exactly what you mean, especially if you've just done a three hour show," Jerry said.

"But I really love to dance," I said. "I just prefer simple two-steps or waltzes. Amateurs always want to show off if they know I'm a dancer-professional. Hey, you're a dancer, let's dance!"

So we did. It was so relaxing and joyous, to just move with the music, doing simple basic dance steps but doing them perfectly. Shirley and Lindsay were dancing, too. We traded partners once or twice.

We hated to go back to do our second show. Somebody later informed me that Lindsay had a crush on me. I didn't know that. One of my roommates in Lake Tahoe, a gorgeous girl named Joy, married Phil Crosby. One of the hardest facts for me to believe now is that all four Crosby boys are gone. How can that be?

My point is, Las Vegas in the Golden Years, was just one long never-failing-never-ending party. Happy time all the time! The hotels were all small compared to today, so there wasn't the long hike trying to get to a restaurant or showroom. That of course, was a factor in the dress code: we all wore high-heels and cocktail clothes weren't out of place, especially at night.

At the Desert Inn we had a wardrobe mistress who was famous and loved for her mothering and advice. Besides looking after our costumes, Virginia looked, on request, after our regular clothes.

One night I remember I put on a cocktail suit Mother made and sent me. It was a really sharp emerald green brocade pencil skirt and long sleeved jacket with portrait collar, very chic. But Virginia took one look and said, "Betty, take off that skirt and give it to me! It's two inches too long! I can't let you go out front looking like that!" She was right, it was. She had it shortened and pressed in ten minutes flat.

Of course, I tipped her $5. I had been worrying about that very thing: that the skirt was too long.

Most of us were fashion plates. All the hotels had dress shops, as they do now, and we often modeled for them, learning what fine clothes felt like.

Showgirls made this town. Oscar Goodman, our good Las Vegas Mayor at the time I'm writing this, makes that statement every chance he gets. We were all over the place due to the casino bosses requirement that showgirls had to "mix." That never bothered me a bit. I would have done it in any case, being too energetic and friendly and hungry for adventure to even think of just sitting in my dressing room between shows or just going home after the midnight show. When I worked as a cocktail lounge singer or floorshow tap act, whichever was available, on the Gulf Coast, the entertainment contracts were always for two weeks with a two week option. If you wanted to be held over you went out of your way to meet and greet and accept drinks and sit down and make friends as much as possible.

It was not "required" it was just common sense. I learned to order Creme De Mint and soda so I wouldn't get tipsy.

Anybody in show business, male or female, learns to charm and work the room, or they don't last very long. Even Broadway stars, too tired to speak, buy the bar a drink at least once in a while. So showgirls learned quickly that it was smart to work the room, especially when bosses grinned ear to ear. We did indeed create Las Vegas. We just didn't realize it at the time.

But I had occasion to see that clearly earlier than most. One afternoon Shecky Green called and invited me to lunch. He said he needed to meet friends at Caesars Palace. I didn't think to ask who were we meeting, so was bowled over to see who was sitting at the table Shecky led me to in the coffee shop. For one thing, I was the only woman and also the only "not famous" one there. Milton Berle held center stage at the table with Corbett Monica, Don Rickles, Pat Cooper, Alan King, Norm Crosby, Joey Villa (not as famous as the others) and Shecky made eight. They pulled up a chair next to Shecky for me, not all the way up to the table. I was ignored from then on, Shecky having introduced me. It was a business meeting.

The Caesars Palace coffee shop had the best Jewish food in the world, the hotel was owned by and catered to Jewish people. Everybody was eating that wonderful food, but they occasionally told jokes since that was their nature. Nobody laughed at the other comedians' jokes, they just nodded, or sometimes helped supply the punch line. Or they added a variation. This was business. The real purpose, as near as I could tell, was to just touch base and talk shop. They apparently all knew each other from the Catskills in Upstate New York, where they had all started when they were young. The Catskills were the best comedians' college in the world.

Then everybody started talking about how many weeks they were booked for in Las Vegas, adding, "I own that room" or "they promised me more weeks next year." The dialog went, "I do eight weeks at the Sahara now, four in the fall, and four in late summer." "I do six weeks at the Trop." "I do three weeks as the opening act in the show-room now." "My agent says I'll get at least six weeks next year." This conversation about how many weeks you spent working in Las Vegas went on for a while. I suddenly realized Las Vegas was prime time for acts. I bit my tongue not to say, Hey fellows, I do fifty-two weeks per year here and have for years. That wouldn't have been appropriate since I was only a dancer, (on the other hand, I was often pulled out of the line to do special business of some kind.) But it did make me aware that having a show business job in Las Vegas on the Strip in a big famous hotel was something rather special. Not just special to dancers, but to all of show business.

I've always felt a kinship and a special affinity for comedians. Know the difference between comedians and comics? Comics say funny things, and comedians say things funny. Anyway, I love all clowns, because they are hiding something sad. Fairly soon after that fabulous lunch, I joined *Bottoms Up* and became a professional comedian/ actress myself, played the Strip for three years, on the road for three more. And I got to dance at the same time. *Bottoms Up* always had dance segments.

All the best comedians are Jewish. You've heard these before, but you can always laugh again...

Why do Jewish divorces cost so much? They're worth it.

I've been in love with the same women for fifty years. If my wife ever finds out, she'll kill me.

What are three words a woman never wants to hear when she's making love? "Honey, I'm home."

We always hold hands. If I let go, she shops.

My wife and I went to a hotel where we got a water bed. My wife called it the Dead Sea.

Why are Jewish men circumcised? Because Jewish women don't like anything that isn't twenty percent off.

Rim shot. Black out. Vamp off.

Chapter 31

Going Bananas

*E*very time I try to tell someone this story, halfway through they stop me with, "Aw come on, Betty, you don't expect me to believe that, do you?" Well actually, I do because every word is true. (as is everything in this book.) It all happened on Friday of the first week of May, 1965. I remember it well because we had to start rehearsal May 10 over in Los Angeles.

About ten months earlier, my little blue Corvair got totaled while I was sitting at a red light in front of the old domed Convention Center on Paradise Road. I was taking my laundry to the laundromat. A lady in a huge black Mercury couldn't/didn't stop, plowed into me, and shoved my car into the car in front of me, squishing my car between them. I broke the steering wheel with my mouth, which opened my lip, had bloody knees and a whiplash. It was worth a tiny story in *Daily Variety* "Show Goes On! Betty Bunch Performs in *Bottoms Up* at the Castaways on the Las Vegas Strip Despite Auto Accident."

Ha. I didn't have any choice. Breck Wall would have killed me if I hadn't been there at show time. Yes, it hurt like hell. You don't know Breck.

Oddly, the car still drove, it just looked awful. The hood, really the trunk in a back engine Corvair was crumpled up six inches and wouldn't go up and wouldn't go down. The engine hatch in back had a gigantic dent which somehow didn't touch the engine. The whole car moved like a crab slightly sideways. My insurance policy didn't have a rental clause so I drove that thing for months until I got a settlement from the Mercury lady. *Bottoms Up* went to Lake Tahoe and I drove the car up there. I drove the wreck back to Las Vegas and days later was hired for a Barry Ashton show going to Japan.

The company of thirty or so dancers, showgirls, assorted singers, and principals all had an enormous amount of preparation to do before departure, getting a passport chief among them. Barry said that we all had to be either redheads or blonds. He also warned us to see our doctors and get a supply of whatever medications we took. I was to be a soloist in one number, so I planned to take jazz classes twice a week at least, to get back in shape from the easy dancing in *Bottoms Up*. Rehearsal was to be in Los Angeles starting Monday, May 10, departure May 21, my birthday.

I decided not to keep my furnished Playpen apartment in Las Vegas as the contract in Japan was for thirteen weeks. So I resolved to pack my belongings and put them in storage. Las Vegas only had one storage facility then, Bekins, on the northwest corner of Charleston Boulevard and Maryland Parkway. My plan was to pack everything, put it into Bekins on Friday, spend Friday and Saturday night next door at my boyfriend's apartment, drive to Los Angeles Sunday, check into a motel, and be ready to start rehearsal Monday morning. One of the other dancers was to room with me in L.A. so we could afford the motel on Beverly Boulevard.

Thursday, the day before D-day was frantic! I had my passport and prescriptions but still had to color my hair red. It was already auburn, but too dark for Barry. Also had to finish packing and go withdraw enough funds from the bank to tide me over until the first paycheck nearly three weeks away. I withdrew $900, all I had, to cover the three weeks.

I also had to cope with a bookcase problem. I owned a wonderful wood bookcase that could be disassembled and stacked. Three seven-foot-long vertical main frames and a seven-foot base piece formed the bookcase. I dismantled that and tied them together with rope then stacked and tied the three-foot shelves in bundles. With my books, full set of china, full set of Revere Ware, kitchen stuff, winter clothes and shoes, linens and blankets, there were seventeen boxes and then the bundles of bookcase parts. Really, too much for the little busted-up Corvair.

But, the next-door boyfriend had a big car and he volunteered to load the boxes and take them to Bekins for me. I warned him that Bekins closed at 5 p.m. sharp on Fridays. He said that he would be home from work by 2 p.m. Friday and we would load and go.

Thursday night I decided to tackle the hair. I am not a hairdresser but Mother owned two beauty shops, and I put my ex-husband through beauty school in Hollywood, so I felt sure I could handle it.

My own hair is auburn, looks dark brown unless I'm in sunlight or spotlight. To change to bright red, you have to bleach out the strands of dark hair starting three fourths of an inch out from the scalp.

Otherwise, the heat of the scalp would make the bleach burn the hair off. When the hair is bleached to "banana yellow," it is then shampooed to remove the bleach, then dried. Then red toner, (which also contains a milder bleach) is applied to roots and strands and they come out the same color all over.

But, Thursday night at midnight having finished the "bleach to banana" part, I was just too tired to finish, so shampooed and dried the ugly bright yellow hair with dark roots and went to bed.

Friday, I finished packing my suitcases to take with me to Los Angeles and on to Japan and took care of details like call Mother and various friends, which of course was very time consuming, and then finished taping up the boxes for storage.

At 2:30 p.m., no boyfriend. I paced the floor 'til 3 p.m., decided I would have to handle it alone and started loading my little car with the seventeen boxes. So, I'm a worry wart.

I opened all the windows and put the bookcase mainframes catty-cornered through the front right window and back left window. They stuck out almost two feet on each side. Two big boxes had to go on top tied down with bungee cords hooked on the open windows. At 4 p.m., I was a nervous wreck. A big wind was up. At 4:15, I tied on a scarf, grabbed my purse and resolving to drive real slow so as not to lose the boxes on top. I went on east down Sierra Vista Drive to Maryland Parkway, where I had to turn right then left around an island in order to go north to Charleston Boulevard to Bekins. As I made that right turn, I heard a sort of whooshing sound and looked in the rear view mirror to see my purse bounce then roll and settle in the middle of Maryland Parkway, opened, with my passport, pill bottles and coin purse into which I had folded $900 dollars: five $100 bills, four $50 bills and ten $20 bills. There also was my billfold with driver's license, without which I couldn't board the plane, all spread across Maryland Parkway's west lane. A couple had already almost reached the purse, a man was only yards away picking up a lipstick case.

I pulled into the left-turn lane at the end of the island, turned off the engine, left the door wide open and sprinted back to my purse, the wind undoing my scarf, screaming, "That's my purse!"

The couple kindly handed me my passport and pill bottles. I picked up my billfold, then the open and empty coin purse. I thanked them and the man. Near tears, I walked the thirty yards back to my car trying to hold down my skimpy little spaghetti strap float-top (under which I was bare) with one hand and holding my cursed purse with the other. My yellow-with-dark-roots hair was standing Medusa-like in the wind. I kept searching the gutter for my money, still holding my purse in one hand and trying to keep my top on with the other. What an unlovely sight I must have been!

Suddenly a voice said, "Miss, is this your car?" A Las Vegas Metropolitan Police Department black and white patrol car had stopped behind the Corvair. I hadn't seen him drive up, I was focusing on the gutter. The handsome young officer was talking to me!

I said, "Yes sir, it is, I'm sorry to have left it in the turn lane, but I had to retrieve my purse."

The officer said, "Where's the other car?"

Long pause. "What other car?" I asked. Long pause.

"Hasn't there been an accident here?" Long pause.

"Oh. Oh no. No, no, oh really officer, my car's damage is from almost a year ago and $900 is missing and Bekins and they close at 5 and I've got to find my money and..."

"Miss, I think you better come sit in the patrol car until I understand this."

"Yes, sir," I said.

Like a gentleman, he opened the patrol car door and helped me in the front seat. Oh, Lord, what if someone I know drives by.

"Now Miss, just tell me slowly what happened."

"Well, officer, I was rear ended almost a year ago, and I am still waiting for the settlement, in the meantime I got a job going to Tokyo and I am trying to get my belongings down to Bekins before they close and I must have left my purse on top of the car I was so frazzled, then it must have fallen off when I turned, and passport, $900, pills, etc. etc. I know I look crazy officer, I'm sorry."

As I talked to him, I glanced out the patrol car window at the desert. We were parked just a little north of Sears, which was the only building there then.

Suddenly, I saw a green bill, slowly turning in the wind, on the other side of the street, in the desert in front of Sears. "There's my money!" I screamed as I opened the patrol car door and ran to the bill only to see another one, then another. The police officer joined me and he, too, started picking up bills. When he found a $100 bill and handed it to me, I whooped with joy, and he laughed, too.

We found and picked up $880. I apologized for looking and sounding like a crazy person and explained about my hair, and said, "I never would have worn this floating short top if I'd known or had time to realize that the wind is up today."

He smiled and wished me a good summer in Japan. I drove home to the Playpen Apartments on Sierra Vista, what else could I do it was 5:10 p.m.

Of course, idiot boyfriend was there and cavalierly said, "I had a drink with the fellows. I'll just drive the boxes down there on Monday. We'll unload your car and put the boxes on the living room floor for the weekend. No problem."

When I arrived back from Japan in September I called that boyfriend to pick me up from the airport as I had sold the little wrecked car in Los Angeles for scrap before we left. You're not going to believe this, but I married Mr. No Show within the year. No excuse. I must have been bananas. He was late or didn't show for the next twenty years.

Who's the idiot now?

Chapter 32

Parker San

In 1965, I lived at the elegant but racy Playpen Apartments on Sierra Vista Drive, famous for all-built-in furniture, very high rent and a nude pool for the showgirls who couldn't get tan lines. I never set foot in that pool. I moved there to be close to my best friends, Teresa and Len Howard, Len being "The Voice of Las Vegas" on radio, everybody's favorite disc jockey. I stood up at their wedding. Teresa worked with me in *Bottoms Up*. They clued me that there was a male resident close to the nude pool who took movies of the girls on the sly through a hole in the fence.

When I got the job going to Japan, I packed up my belongings for storage before going to LA for rehearsal. We left from Los Angeles May 21, my birthday.

The flight to Japan was horrendously long. Eighteen hours with one brief hour stop in Honolulu. Back in the air, the darling stews celebrated my birthday with petite fours in a big pyramid circle on a big round tray, with candles. Birthday cards were improvised with vomit bags and crayons. The entire company, thirty strong, sang, "Happy Birthday."

It was fun and sweet, but I brooded for the rest of the trip. Except for the company manager, I was, at thirty-one, the oldest in the company.

The girl on my left was seventeen, and had to get special parental permission papers to make the trip. The girl across the aisle was eighteen. I think this was the start of my baby panic that became full-blown that fall. I had been, like Scarlett, going to "think about that tomorrow" for years. I felt old and tired, and I already knew everything there was to know about chorus dancing. The young girls always asked me about counts, placement, makeup, how to do your hair, etc. Not much challenge left for me.

The owners and bookers from our big, elegant nightclub, The Latin Quarter in the Akasaki District, met us with a two-dozen bouquet of American Beauty roses each and took us via charter bus directly to an afternoon cocktail party at the club. They served up champagne, heavy canapés and a jazz trio. Unfortunately, the food included raw chunks of bloody tuna, a delicacy that I found nauseating after an eighteen-hour flight, or any time for that matter! I still can't do sushi to this day. You had to see the blood dripping off the chins to understand. And the air of Tokyo smelled funny to me. I was told the cooking gas was different from ours, a propane or something, and it made the entire atmosphere, along with all that fish, smell not so good to me. It took about a week to get used to it.

My dear friend from a year at the Riviera, Gayle Ravese, and I taxied after the party to the New Otani Hotel, where Barry Ashton Productions, our employer, had made reservations. (By the way, Gayle is still a good friend, some forty-two years later. She's still in Las Vegas, and owns an antiques shop). Our room in the hotel was miniature everything — a condition we found ever-present the entire summer. Later, we moved to the Nikatsu Hotel in the Ginza, an older hotel with huge rooms, very homey and close to shopping. In fact, the Nikatsu basement had a great shopping area — china, linens, clocks, tchotchkes. I bought a glass-domed clock to send home to Mother and watched the man nail together a wooden box on the spot to ship it in.

But I learned to love the clever Japanese early that first morning. We woke up to discover it was raining, hard and steady, and we had to get to rehearsal. We ordered coffee and pineapple juice (having been clued that it was cheap and orange juice was canned and expensive). Shortly after it arrived, there was a gentle tap tap tap at the door. There stood a nice Japanese lady holding up six raincoats for us to choose from for $7 each — black, tan or gray. I wore that beautifully made, shiny black cotton coat for years and it doubled as an evening coat. Gayle bought one, too, as did nearly all the girls. Later on, we bought fabric and had suits made to measure. Tokyo has great tailors.

The second week we were there, who should show up ringside but Steve Parker, Parker San, himself ("san" is Japanese for Mr.). One of the boy dancers and three girls, besides myself, were in the Parker-Lee Productions show that never opened at the Aladdin. We knew Steve, Shirley MacLaine's husband, lived in Tokyo, but didn't realize that he would come see the new American show in town and recognize all of us. He sent word backstage asking "his dancers" to join him for a drink out front between shows. The others rushed to dress and go, jockeying to get to sit next to the charming and handsome Steve. I took my time freshening up and sauntered out to find Steve had saved the place next to him for me because I reminded him of Shirley, he said, which I still think of as one of the nicest things anybody has ever said to me. I'm a huge fan of hers. Actually, we are the same age (she's three weeks older), same height, same dancing background, same mother/teacher who wanted to be an actress herself. I now belong to the same church as she does, Science of Mind. Now you can make fun of me, too.

Steve showed up at the Latin Quarter about once a week after that first evening to take the five of us out for drinks and supper. He called a couple of times at the hotel to make sure I was available, once asking if we would all come out to the house after the last show for a party. Putting the boy dancer in the front with the driver still left five of us for the small Mercedes-Benz sedan backseat. This led to lots of giggles and Steve insisting I sit on his lap. It was a forty-five minute ride out to the suburbs. (I was terrified I might toot).

It was a beautiful Japanese-style house, complete with a tranquil Zen Garden, which Steve showed me alone. We returned to the party and he took my hand and said, "I want to show you something, shh, shh," and led me to the bedroom wing into his beautiful little sleeping daughter's room that was dimly lit with her nightlite. He was obviously so proud of their baby, who lived with him while Shirley traveled making movies. And the little girl was darling, seven or eight I guessed, blonde, pixie face, cuddling her dolly. We tiptoed back to the party. I was touched. (More baby panic?)

Once on our dark night, Steve asked me to dinner without the others and took me to the Friars Club, a famous theatrical private club with branches all over the world.

Another time, at a restaurant with all six of us, we really had tons of food and drink. When presented with the complicated bill, Steve frowned and handed it to me, followed by a tossed coin purse stuffed full of large Japanese bills and said, "You take care of it, Betty." In Japan, men never bother with money or checks — it's considered beneath them. Wives handle all that. I was very flattered. I never even got pinned in high school. Sigh.

We half-learned three shows in Los Angeles, each to be done for four weeks. Midsummer, we were in afternoon rehearsals for one of the alternate shows we would be putting on soon. I didn't mention to Steve that I was doing a solo turn in the new show, a barroom Gay

Nineties song and dance, "May I Tempt You With a Big Red Rosy Apple" (Cause you're the apple of my eye, oh my!), in which I threw plastic red apples to the audience and called out silly remarks such as "Run to the round-house, Sister, they can't corner you there!" I wore a scanty black lace corset chemise, black net hose, and black heels.

One afternoon, Steve showed up at rehearsal and came unglued when I did my little comedy act, saying, "Why didn't you tell me you were doing a solo? Why didn't you let me know? You're a star!" I was surprised to learn he was interested in my career.

When we talked about it, like that I had been a tap act in New Orleans between semesters at the University of Texas, he offered me a job at $1,000 a week (a fortune) in his nightclub in Vietnam. He said I didn't have to strip, just wear scanty costumes and dance, nothing I would be uncomfortable doing. Saigon was still being bombed occasionally in 1965, and I chickened out. I should have done it. I'd be a wealthy woman today. Come to think of it, I am wealthy, because I'm happy with what I have. Steve Parker was a fabulous man. I certainly see what Miss MacLaine saw in him. I'm sorry it didn't work out for them. Or me.

Chapter 33

Kasiwada

One of the silly remarks I made doing my little solo comedy number in Tokyo was, "I want a Sumo wrestler! Bring me a Sumo wrestler!"

In modern Japan, the Geisha tradition has been replaced with hostesses, lovely ladies in modern dress who join gentlemen's tables by request, then entertain with jokes. Some specialize in dirty jokes, stories, table tricks (like palmistry or origami), and charm. They also turn on a little light when the table needs service. They are paid by the hour, often with big tips added if they are extra beautiful or extra charming. And boy do they dress — very expensively with beautifully matching shoes, bag, jewelry.

So, some of the hostesses, who were there every night, got together and did, indeed, surprise me with a Sumo wrestler for me! They said he was a friend of one of the hostesses. He was a grand champion named Kashiwada, which I understood meant candy box in Japanese. He wore a traditional Japanese kimono, a sash, and sandals. His skin (forearms and face were all I could see) was like velvet — massaged, he later told me, with sandalwood oil daily after his workout, followed by a steam bath and a hot tub. His long hair was slicked back into a short ponytail, again polished with sandalwood oil. Oh, did he smell divine. But it was fairly clear from the start that he wasn't interested in me, girlfriendwise. Or, at least he never flirted or had busy hands. He was a little reserved yet friendly.

At the end of the first evening, I sat at his table. After we said good night, he stopped briefly to speak with his friend the hostess. Then she followed me on my way backstage, stopped me and gave me two Japanese bills I recognized as the equivalent of $20 each. I said, "No, no! Why is he giving me money? I can't take that."

She later explained it was customary to pay hostesses, in the Geisha tradition, for their company and conversation. She also explained that he would be insulted if I refused the money and would certainly not come back.

So, I became a Geisha. From then on, my Sumo wrestler came to see me once a week between shows and stayed for the last show. He waited for me, bought me a drink or two then said a sedate and polite good night, leaving my "fee" with his friend to be given to me. Forty extra a week isn't exactly chopped liver! And he was fun to be around, very educational.

As we got to know each other, I learned my Sumo wrestler was worried about his weight, he told me. He was underweight at six-foot two-inches and 240 pounds. I thought he was gorgeous, like a University of Texas Longhorn fullback. He ordered a fifth of Martell Cordon Bleu cognac and a pound of butter cut into patties with a toothpick in each patty. Then he had a patty of butter, and as it melted in his mouth, a shot of cognac to wash it down. He always finished the bottle and the pound of butter with no visible effect.

His English was very good, and as I said, he was fun to talk to. I asked him how he won Sumo matches if he was underweight. He explained it wasn't all about weight. That leverage played a large part, the trick being to use the opponent's weight against him.

About his third visit, in conversation, I discovered he had done his junior year at Purdue University, and was a graduate engineer. Slow as I am, I finally realized he came to see me to practice his English, as well as seek company while he worked at gaining weight.

One evening, the dance band was playing a Gershwin ballad and I impulsively asked Kashi if he would dance with me. He hesitated only a second, then did so. He had a pretty good slow dance. Later, the hostesses told me that was a shocking sight. Sumos never do anything untraditional in public. They are considered the "keepers of the old ways." As a grand champion, Kashiwada was a national hero.

The last week we were there, he came in one night, sent the captain backstage to fetch me as usual, but met me in the lobby instead of waiting for me to be brought to his booth.

He said, "Betty, this is a very special evening. I've brought someone to meet you," gesturing to the most exquisitely beautiful creature I ever laid eyes on. She was dressed in an all-white, traditional kimono and an elaborate brocade Obi with touches of pink. Her tiny feet were slipped into white tabbies and platform sandals. She wore rice powder on her perfect porcelain skin and her black hair was pulled softly back in several chignons with traditional white pearl combs that looked like real pearls. She looked perhaps sixteen or seventeen years old, as was her waist in inches. She bowed to me almost all the way to the floor. I smilingly bowed back, not very deeply, apologizing for my lack of manners as a foreigner (a mannerly touch I had learned).

Kashi then introduced her aunt who doubled as her chaperone. Likewise, she was also traditionally dressed in a somber gray kimono. Evidently, the evening had been an engagement party or something of that nature.

The fiancée and the aunt were led to a booth, Kashi and I were seated nearby but out of hearing distance.

Of course, I requested information on the wedding, which I learned was to be held three months hence, he said. Kashi told me all about it — a big, formal, traditional event. He said his fiancée had been "dying to meet me," the famous American entertainer.

It was hard to say goodbye to Kashi. I'd become fond of him. He was a worthy national hero.

In Japan, I am told, the lower the bow, the more respect is being shown. However, it is an insult to bow deeply if it isn't appropriate for the person's status.

So, was Kashi's fiancée honoring me, or insulting me with that deep bow? Nah.

That child was too beautiful to have ever had a mean thought. May they now and forever be happy. Forty-three years ago, seems like yesterday.

Today's dancers, as well as those of the late 1960s and all years in between, often catch jobs going to Japan, Paris, Brazil, or wherever. We were the first company, I believe, that went to Japan.

Las Vegas dancers have become a very sophisticated group. Am I sophisticated? You betcha, I am. Heck, ya'll, I'm a Geisha!

Chapter 34

Dorothy Dorben Dancers

In the fall of 1965, there was a dancers wanted audition notice in the paper for the Aladdin hotel, Dorothy Dorben, choreographer. I'd been out of work for six weeks, the longest I'd ever gone without finding work. Lots of American dancers were out of work because we had three French shows running: *Lido de Paris*, *Folies Bergere* and *Casino de Paris*. They all used English or French girls as a general rule. Dorben was well known; she had the line at the El Rancho for years, but I had never worked or even auditioned for her.

So, I got out my dance shoes, the two-inch heeled ones called "character shoes" that had rubber soles and were suitable for jazz, found my ballet shoes to take just in case, chose a black leotard with long sleeves, checked all my black, sheer dance hose for a good pair and packed an audition bag. Mine was a black nylon duffel bag.

It contained all the things a dancer might need at an audition: Tylenol, quinine tablets for leg cramps, a small towel, a comb, extra hair pins and nets, a hand mirror (fairly large), eau de toilette of some kind, tissue, a nail file, Band-Aids and, depending on what the audition notice said, high-heeled pumps (in case they wanted to see a showgirl walk). If tap shoes were required, it would be good to have a very small screw-driver to tighten the taps if necessary. And, very important, a head shot and resume stapled together.

I'm usually excited at an audition but not dry-mouthed nervous like I was as a beginner. But I was very nervous at this one because I really needed the job. So were all my dancer friends. We were all in the same boat, resulting in a huge turnout, at least eighty auditioners!

The thing was, the huge number of us discombobulated Miss Dorben; she evidently hadn't realized there were that many out-of-work dancers in Las Vegas. She had us flap-ball-change across the stage three at a time on the diagonal, then same formation, but jete, waltz, turn, pique, turn. Then she called a lineup, which had to be three deep. We all stood there a long time before she said, "Thank you" and walked away. Was the audition over?

She hadn't picked anyone. We milled around for a while, visiting with each other.

The next day, I called friends in Los Angeles, as well as Las Vegas, and eventually (it took a while) found out the poor lady was overwhelmed, according to her assistants, and just couldn't decide what to do.

Over the next week, I was on the phone daily until I found out she was having another audition in Los Angeles. I also found out that she had actually hired girls from that audition that she knew because they had worked for her before — one of them being a friend of mine, who immediately clued me in on the above information and suggested I drive to L.A. and attend the audition. So, I did, and got the job.

We rehearsed a week at the Coronet Theater in West Hollywood. I stayed with my old friend Chris, who I always stayed with in L.A. She was at the Moulin Rouge with me for four years, then with Tony Martin at the Copacabana in New York. Friends are a tremendous asset in any business, but in dancing they are indispensable. If the other girls don't like you, look out.

The problem with this rehearsal was that I was really out of shape. I should have been taking class the last six weeks. It was entirely my own fault and, boy, did I pay. I hurt from head to toe. Further, I began to realize that age was definitely a factor. I was one of the older girls there. In fact, Miss Dorben's first assistant was a girl that had worked in the line with me, now considered herself too old and out of shape to perform, and she was my age, exactly.

As the assistant took notes and brought coffee, I told her I was really hurting and worried. She then scared me to death, saying, "Yes, we are worried about you, too."

Yikes! What does that mean? I thought.

I was taking a dancer's bath every night after rehearsal. Many dancers swear it helps sore muscles. The recipe includes pouring a small bottle of baby oil, a small bottle of iodine, and two to three cups of Epsom salts into a bath of hot, running water.

Then stay immersed as long as you can. I swear by it, especially if you add two ounces of Scotch. Not in the bath silly! Campho-Phenique can substitute for the iodine.

Such dance workouts produce small foot blisters, scratches, and maybe even muscle strains that are helped with this treatment. Best of all is a massage, but I was usually too tired and too broke.

Sleep is the best medicine. But, oh, how it hurts to get up. You literally have to allow extra time to get ready in the morning.

I called Mother looking for sympathy, I suppose, and got none. "You insisted on a dancing career; now you have to pay the price," she said.

She was right, of course.

If you take two dance classes a week like any dancer is supposed to, you won't get so sore. Ballet companies start each day, even on the road, with an hour barre.

Over the years, I've used these experiences to counsel young people when they tell me they want to be an actress/singer/dancer.

When you think you want to be a performer, I tell them, you need to consider whether or not you really want to "be one, " or do you perhaps really just want to do what actresses do or have what actresses have?

If so, maybe what you really want is fame. Maybe what you really want is lots of money. Maybe what you really want is to hang out with famous people.

If so, there are many ways to be famous, like discover a cure for cancer or write a best-seller, or find the lost continent of Atlantis. There are also, of course, many ways to get rich. And, if you want to do what performers do, there's always local theater or a church choir.

If you want to hang out with famous people, then learn wardrobe, makeup, or photography, or be a stagehand or a party-planner, or theatrical agent.

But if you really want to be an actress/singer/dancer, you're going to have to pay the price, including spending hours all alone memorizing lines, or hours working at a ballet barre, or hours doing vocal exercises. You will turn down dates because you can't stay out late since you're in rehearsal. You may have to move away from your family to go where theatrical work is found. To be a professional performer, you'll sometimes need to give interviews when you don't feel like it — try being charming sometime when you have a bad headache.

You might have to sign autographs for ninety people when you're tired and hungry. You might have to lose five pounds by opening night (I'm very familiar with that one!)

You have to take the good with the bad. Forgive the cliché, but young folks often don't think there is a bad side to professional performing other than the glamorous-sounding nuisance of the paparazzi so glorified in the current press.

Fortunately, for me, I've always loved the actual work of rehearsal, loved ballet and tap classes. Even auditioning finally became something I actually loved doing. I loved the challenge.

This Dorothy Dorben show, *The Jet Set Revue*, opened with a great jazz number done to *The African Waltz*, which is unusual because it's in 5/4 time. Not a problem for me. We loved the costume — solid pink sequined stretch jump suits with pink leather boots.

But the big closing number was the dreaded cancan. As usual, the skirts were solid ruffles and very heavy, and we did, indeed, have a jump-split at the end. Three girls had to do the split, so we alternated so we really only had to do it maybe three to four times per week.

When it was my turn, I had to warm up for half an hour. It was a fun show to do, dear girlfriends were made, but I began to realize I was getting past dancing prime and better start thinking ahead as to what else I could do — a heartbreaking time for a dancer.

Further, at thirty-one, I was feeling baby panic, and as they say, the clock was ticking.

Providential good luck has been a hallmark of my career. At the end of *The Jet Set Revue*, (I think we ran three months), Breck Wall turned up and wanted me back in *Bottoms Up*. He had a contract for the Thunderbird Hotel, where we stayed a year, doing two shows per afternoon (nights off!), playing to standing-room only audiences.

I got married during that year, 1966, got pregnant, danced in the show until I was almost seven months along and returned after I had my Rick to play the show for another year.

I am very grateful for all these blessings, and for many more that were yet to come.

Chapter 35

Las Vegas Movies

*R*ain Man was on television last week. Wasn't it fun to see the older Caesars Palace? And it's a terrific movie. I recognized some of our local actors working, always a good thing. But there is, sadly, another lost cause. Movies are still done here (no Hollywood set of Las Vegas ever looks real to me), but they don't hire local actors anymore. Just extras. And, they always tell the local production people they don't want anyone over forty on the set.

Now, when Charlene Goldman (Judge Paul Goldman's wife) ran the movie industry here in the late seventies and eighties, the production companies did hire local actors. Me, for instance. Charlene had worked for Aaron Spelling in Los Angeles and knew the industry very well. She did everything — locations, casting, wardrobe — you name it. When and if the movie was too big to handle all that by herself, she hired Maggie Mancuso to assist her. Margaret Ann Peterson, Maggie, was Andy Griffith's girlfriend, one of the "Darlings" on *The Andy Griffith Show*. If the project was even bigger, Charlene called in Jody Sloat. If the two of them were not enough, she called me in. I usually checked in extras, lots of paperwork there. I had listed myself with her agency as an actress, so she found out I had worked as a dancer on all those old fifties musicals and TV shows, and had also done parts on *77 Sunset Strip* and others. When *Going in Style*, starring George Burns, came to town in 1979, I read for a part and got it, so Charlene knew I was a professional. Movie sets have very strict rules and customs, and nobody tells you what they are, you just have to know from experience.

For instance, if you're on time, you're late.

In 1981, *Lookin' to Get Out*, directed by Hal Ashby and starring Jon Voight, came to town and had a huge scene to be done in the Stardust showroom with Siegfried & Roy. I got a tiny role.

Siegfried & Roy had the tigers out running on the circular runway in the audience for the scene. They always had done that, every night during their regular show, no problem. But without huge movie lights on stilts, focused on the runway, shining in their eyes. One of the tigers was spooked and jumped off the runway out into the audience of extras. It was incredibly sudden and incredibly scary.

Roy yelled the one word that would control the situation: What do you think that would be? He yelled "Freeze!" Three-hundred people did so.

Terrified people will do what they are told. I was a good forty feet away from the animal, but others could have reached out and touched it. All holding our breath, we watched Roy slowly, softly approach the tiger, talking to it calmly and steadily.

Meanwhile, four men dressed in black and holding chains with locks, very quietly stalked up behind the tiger. When Roy reached the big cat and grasped its collar, they pounced, in an obviously rehearsed move, to chain and secure, two on each side pulling opposite each other to completely control the poor, scared animal. One of the assistant directors quickly said, "Lunch." And we all filed out, glad to be alive, about half in shock.

After lunch, the same shot had to be done, only the extras sitting at the table right under the runway where the tiger jumped off refused to sit there. Charlene calmly said, "No problem, I'll sit there," and did so, shaming others to join her and finish the scene. What a day.

Still a legend in the biz, it's called, "The day the tiger got loose."

Even more fun was 1982's *Starman*, with John Carpenter directing and Jeff Bridges starring. It was a very big deal, and they planned to hire several local actors. I read for and got the role of the truck-stop waitress — the second one, not to be confused with the first waitress in the film, where the Starman revived the dead deer. Every actress in town tried for the role. I was working a high heels-and-suit job at the time, in the convention industry. My second callback was at the Tropicana. I brought a suitcase to work that day, loaded with my waitress outfit — a blue-and-white-check cotton dress from Kmart, a plain white apron, a man's brown dowdy sweater and beat-up brown loafers. At the Trop, I went into the ladies room and put it all on, wiping off my bright red lipstick and messing up my chic hair. Charlene said to the Hollywood casting director, "I see Betty is in her method actress mode." I got the role to be shot a week away.

In the meantime, Charlene had to cast and set up a huge Interstate 15 highway scene. She got Governor Richard Bryan to have the Nevada Highway Patrol close Interstate 15 for a one-mile stretch out between Boulder City and Hoover Dam or thereabouts.

She gave me the job of calling and handling fifty members of the Nevada National Guard. Charlene got the list of guardsmen, somehow. I called them all to book them, then had to call them back about what uniform they were to wear, then called again about where to meet me.

Three days before the highway shoot, Charlene called me and said, "You have to work the shot. I want you to bring your husband, your two sons, your Blazer pulling your boat, with bicycles tied on top, along with several pieces of luggage and your dog Queenie on a leash. It will pay lots because everything will be paid for, including the suitcases and the dog."

I said, "Charlene, I can't work the shot. What if the director or one of his assistants sees me? They'll take away my part!"

That's called "established," and is a no-no.

"So, wear a wig with a scarf over it, big dark glasses, a big heavy jacket with a pulled-up collar and stay away from the assistants and the camera," she said. "I need you, and you have to be there anyway to check in the National Guard."

Charlene was not a person to whom you said no.

Late in the afternoon, the assistant directors called everyone over to line each side of the highway. Wouldn't you know, they placed Jeff Bridges in character not thirty feet away from me. To my horror, I realized it was to be a three-camera shot with one camera on a boom moving overhead. This shot turned into one of my best acting gigs ever. How to keep your face out of all three cameras was a worthy challenge, to be sure. We rehearsed the shot once and I spotted my best friends Jody and Maggie standing out of range dying with laughter and enjoying my creative choreography and long face.

As camera one focused on Jeff Bridges and those of us close to him, I searched through my purse — head down, of course — looking for a Kleenex, turning slightly away, back to the wind. As camera two focused on the National Guard running up the highway past me, I had to blow my nose with a handful of Kleenex hiding my face. As camera three swung overhead, I accidentally dropped my purse and had to turn away and half squat to retrieve it. It was masterful, if I do say so myself. Whew!

The next week, I was flown in a private jet carrying other personnel from Las Vegas down to Holbrook, Arizona, for my big scene with

Karen Allen. I was escorted in a Teamsters sedan to the set to my own private dressing room with my name on the door. I got dressed immediately and went early to the set inside a real truck-stop diner so I could get my bearings.

Suddenly, Miss Allen was on the set, and an assistant director introduced me to her. John Carpenter came over to me, smiled and asked, how was the flight, was I feeling OK, any questions? If not, then, let's rehearse it. We did the scene. He said that's fine, let's shoot it. We did so. He said let's do it again. I asked if there was anything he wanted changed. He said no, that was perfect, just do it that way again. We did it six times, same question from me and same answer from him every time.

Then he came over to me and said, "Thank you. You were perfect. You're wrapped."

There is always this terrible let-down feeling after a day like that. I drove home, stopped at Safeway and made dinner for my family. A neighbor from across the street waved.

Don't these people know who I am?

with John Voight

Chapter 36

Happy Daze

*T*elevision's influence on our lives in America intensified in the seventies. *Happy Days*, the Fonz, *Laverne & Shirley*, "jumping the shark," the names Ron Howard, and Henry Winkler all became household names in the culture and remained so for decades.

By 1984 my acting career was bigger than my dancing career. I had a Hollywood agent, and burned up the highway to L.A. two, sometimes three times per month. I drove a 1969 Cadillac convertible with a 600 horsepower engine, so I felt safe and protected on the highway.

I can't resist a little side-bar here: that car was incredible, turquoise with white ostrich leather upholstery and every expensive option available. Joel and I bought it in 1972, three years old and perfect. We found the previous owner's papers in the glove compartment. New, it had belonged to Mr. Lefthand Thunderbolt of Tulsa, Oklahoma. Obviously a wealthy Osage Native American. I loved that car. I raised my sons in that car. When the cloth top wore out, I had the whole car reconditioned at Cashman Cadillac, new top and motor, fresh blue corduroy upholstery and paint. It was great!

The tires had white sidewalls. After I moved to Hollywood people followed me (or it) down the street asking if they could buy it. Even on the freeway. That car, even after it got old, made me feel rich.

So, my agent called one morning and said I had gotten a reading tomorrow morning for *Mr. Sunshine*, a new sitcom at Universal starring Jeffery Tambor, produced by Henry Winkler. The story about a blind man's problems living his life was eventually canceled due to too many mistaken identity jokes.

I was there at the appointed hour, wondering who I'd be reading for, nearly died when it turned out to be Henry Winkler himself. There was another actress there, and I nearly died again when she threw her arms around Mr. Winkler, saying, "Darling, how have you been!" and he answered, "Great, how about you, Ruth?" Not a good sign.

She read first, while I studied the dialogue. It was obvious to me that the piece needed a triple take, a seldom performed burlesque trick, three takes in a row, and a pretty gutsy thing to try. But I was so sure that's what it needed, I resolved to do it.

I read with an assistant with Mr. Winkler sitting on a couch to watch.

When we finished, he got up, took the script out of the assistant's hand and said he wanted to read with me! I must have done something right. We read it, me still doing the triple take. At the end, he had a big grin on his face and said, "Betty, you've got the role." I was so thrilled. They don't usually tell you on the spot. He walked me down to meet the director, John Rich, and said wardrobe would call me, rehearsal was the next day at 10 a.m. on the Universal lot.

The next day, I met the rest of the cast, Jeffrey Tambor was especially charming. We rehearsed in the same room for two more days. On the third day, my call was later than the others. I had sat down at the table to watch the scene being rehearsed, and Mr. Winkler arrived, said hello to me and sat down, too, but he was scowling and not happy.

Suddenly, he was on his feet, moving around the table picking up empty chip sacks, paper plates, crumpled napkins, half-eaten apples, ice-cream sticks, and ashtrays overflowing. He poured water on the ashtrays to be sure they were dead, then dumped everything in a large trash can in the corner. He didn't do this silently; it was all accompanied by deep sighs, and heavy breathing.

As our star producer dampened a paper towel and started wiping down the table, the rehearsing actors took a break, and intuitively realizing that something was amiss, quietly and silently gathered around the table.

"I'm really upset with all of you," Henry Winkler said. "Well, Betty just got here. This room looks like a pigsty. Can't any of you clean up after yourselves? This room is a theater, as is any rehearsal area.

"The theater is my home, and I resent anybody who doesn't respect my home. Is it asking too much to request that you clean up after your coffee breaks? The theater is my home and my life's work and my love. And, as professionals, you should feel that way too, or get out of the business."

Out came such a chorus of: "I'm so sorry. It will never happen again. I would have cleaned it up, but didn't want to risk making noise (this from me.) I'm so sorry."

Mr. Winkler then graciously said, "OK. I've had my say. Now let's get on with rehearsal. You're all wonderful artists, and I forgive you."

I love to tell this story to young performers after I've asked them to please pick up their messes. The theater is my home, too.

Chapter 37

Oxford Blues

*B*ack in 1984, Charlene Goldman was the "Movie Lady" here in Las Vegas. She had worked for Aaron Spelling in Los Angeles and knew all elements of the business — wardrobe, catering, props, locations, makeup and hairdressing, Teamsters, etc. I had listed myself with her agency as an actress, as had Maggie Peterson and Jody Sloat, but since the three of us had long resumes and years of experience working in film, she called us in to work production when she couldn't handle everything herself. We all became close friends.

One day we were together in Charlene's office, when she told us she had an exciting project on the way into town. It was a major film, starring Rob Lowe, called *Oxford Blues*. The company was in London finishing up the story and had most of the film in the can, with only the opening segment and some hotel scenes yet to be done. Char felt sure there would be small roles to be cast here and assured us we would get to read for them. The location was to be the Dunes Hotel. Rob's part was as a valet and University of Nevada, Las Vegas, rowing star who heads off to Oxford.

The Dunes also would be the "home" hotel, with the entire company staying there. The first two days would be at Lake Mead, as part of the story involved the rowing team.

There were complicated location plans to be made. Charlene told us to stand by and said she'd be in touch.

Two or three days later my phone rang at 7 p.m. It was Maggie, saying she had Jody on a conference call and that we had decisions to make. Charlene was too busy to call each of us. Members of the *Oxford Blues* company had arrived. There were no roles to be cast except college-age men for the UNLV rowing team. All they needed were production people, wardrobe, script supervisor, hair and makeup and a few IATSE (stagehands).

Charlene felt so badly about there being no roles for us, said Maggie, that she had decided that we would be the production people! Further, Charlene got on the phone, saying, "OK, who wants to be what? You're actresses, you can do this! Maggie will do wardrobe. That's the hardest. Which one of you owns a hot roller set?"

I said, "I do."

Charlene said, "OK, you're the hairdresser. Oh, don't worry. There is only one actress, and she has shoulder-length hair worn down. Easy. Jody, that leaves you to be the script supervisor."

Maggie said, "Yes, and Jody has one of those timer things to go around the neck to time scenes."

Jody said, "Yes, but Betty just gave me the Script Supervisor book. She's read it, but I haven't."

Charlene interrupted, "So she'll tell you what to do. Mags and Betty, meet me in the Dunes coffee shop at 3 p.m. tomorrow. I'll give you the cast list and sizes of the rowing team. Betty, you don't start 'til the scenes at the Dunes, so you'll be Maggie's assistant until then. She'll really need help."

Jody called me first thing the next morning. I told her the script supervisor simply keeps a written record of the shots so the editor can make sense out of miles of film before him on reels. Like: Scene One, Take One: Airplane overhead, bad sound. Take Two: Actor missed line. Cut. Take Three: Good take. Print. Take Four: Also good take. Print for insurance.

The supervisor sits in a camp chair (usually), right next to the camera. Jody was perfect and looked the role, too, sun hat, sunglasses, expensive timer and all.

We met Charlene in the coffee shop and panicked at the list of needs for the next morning.

One little item: eighteen UNLV Rebels hooded sweats for the rowing team. Rob's character was a champion rowing captain; that, and a few computer tricks helped him get into Oxford.

When we found out about the hoodies, Maggie looked at her watch and gasped, "Oh, no! Wonderworld (which we knew carried UNLV sweats) closes in twenty minutes!"

We sprinted to valet, got my car, dashed to Wonderworld (corner of Spring Mountain and Maryland Parkway) over the speed limit and screeched to a halt in front to let Maggie out. I barely got my car parked and ran in the front door as the manager was walking up with the keys to close the store.

We frantically found assorted sizes in Rebels hoodies, then did the same in black pants.

We had to dress several valets for background. Rob's character met a female benefactor when he valet parked her car. Maggie and I then hot-footed at 9:30 p.m. to Saks Fifth Avenue to find an evening dress and robe for our actress, Gail Strickland, who turned out to be silent and cooperative. Maggie grabbed several great cocktail dresses and a beautiful $250 robe. I went home, as part of my job was to open the door to the makeup/hair room at 6 a.m. It was already late.

Maggie called me at 5 a.m. to say, "Are you set? Got props? Don't forget a vanity mirror for the set."

Thank goodness I actually had one (a ten-inch mirror with a longish handle to hold in front of the actress before her scene for confidence). I had stopped at the drug store the night before and bought several types of hairspray and new brushes and combs and a cloth cape.

I said, "Have you got your ironing board and iron?" Maggie gasped, "No! I forgot that. Do you have one I can borrow?"

"Sure, I do," I said. "I'll bring it."

After I opened the door every morning, my first job was to call room service for coffee and Danish, enough for a dozen people. Oh, did I love that!

Rob was usually the first actor there, sleep still in his eyes. He got coffee, then sat in his makeup chair, throwing off a, "Good morning, everybody." Sweet boy.

I had told my actress (as I had been told many times) to arrive "clean and rolled," so getting her ready involved just brushing it out upside down, lightly spraying and going to the set.

I packed up my hot rollers (to be used as the day progressed), my kit with hairspray, brushes and combs and headed with the rest of the crew to the set. The director introduced himself, called me by name, and got on with it.

I kept my rollers hot all day, remembering to unplug them once in a while to cool off from burning hot. After every "cut, reset " I went to Gail to check her out, mirror in hand, fluffing out her hair as necessary. She was very good.

On wrap night, Charlene insisted we join her for dinner at the Dome of the Sea, the Dunes' very expensive seafood restaurant. She ordered champagne and said, "Order anything you want. Make it expensive — the company is paying."

Oh, did we have fun. I had lobster thermidor.

A week or so later, Charlene called us in to see and read a letter from the *Oxford Blues* company. It thanked her for all her help, and added, "We were especially pleased with your wonderful production people. They were so efficient and professional."

We screamed with laughter until we had to sit.

Chapter 38

Bluebells

My friend Pam Kreishenbaumer is the quintessential Bluebell dancer, one of those who went back and forth between London, Paris, and Las Vegas, dancing for Donn Arden and Miss Bluebell in the late fifties and sixties. The girls were called Bluebells because the London talent agency that kept them working was owned by a woman whose eyes were the exact shade of blue, as were the famous English countryside blossoms called bluebells.

Miss Bluebell was famous not only for the tall, talented beauties she found, but for her motherly concern for her girls to mix, meaning go out front and look pretty. She had no problem with nudity, just mixing. American girls had no problem with mixing, but, for the most part, disparaged nudity, since we tend to think of nudity in connection with burlesque and vulgarity. This pretty much changed in the late sixties when, as I've talked about before, silicone breast implants or direct injections became available. And Americans soon realized there was nothing at all vulgar about Arden's nudes. He wouldn't allow it. He dictated no "jiggling," no spit curls, no colored eye shadow except natural, meaning gray or brown. I well remember his yelling from the back of the house to some hapless nude dancer, "Stiffen your back, you're jiggling!" And Miss Bluebell only represented young ladies who had ballet training and a certain class.

Many Bluebells fell in love, married and stayed here, and can be found all over town, teaching school, selling real estate, running dance/ballet schools, participating in our communities and gracing our cultural organizations in the time-honored English way.

The Bluebells came to Las Vegas in 1958 in the *Lido de Paris* at the Stardust, while I was working for Arden myself, but at the Moulin Rouge in Hollywood. They stayed for years at the Stardust until replaced by *Enter the Night*, which never attained the legendary status of the *Lido* shows.

One little discouraging word, usually never heard from me: In 1964, I was out of work for three months, as were all my dancer friends. The English line captains, responsible for auditioning and hiring replacements, wouldn't hire American dancers. The three biggest shows in town, *Lido* at the Stardust, *Casino de Paris* at the Dunes and the *Folies Bergere* at the Tropicana, were all cast with European, Australian, French or English dancers, and they wanted to hire their mates to work with. It seems like the same situation now exists with Cirque du Soleil.

It's been a longtime dream of mine and my fellow retired-by-age dancer/showgirls, to be able to do a senior revue, like the highly successful *Palms Springs Folies*, but without having to move to Palm Springs. There was lots of talk, even a few meetings toward that end over the last few years.

In early November, two Bluebell dancers, each more beautiful and talented than the other, Liz Lieberman and Lesley Bandy, actually achieved that impossible dream. There was no audition, the gypsy phone tree went into action and about twenty tappers showed up for Rick Rizzo's tap class, and opened the show that developed. Rizzo had been asked to create the opening number. Liz and Lesley made places for all of us. And, on November 4, we performed *Las Vegas Legends* at The Orleans Showroom.

I meant to tap dance, but took a spill on the first day of rehearsal and quickly became a showgirl by default. We had so much fun. We laughed and giggled and hooted.

I was so busy talking and joking that I didn't learn the showgirl routine until the last run-through before showtime. We only had one morning in The Orleans Showroom, however, the show was a success with all the bills paid and $7,000 donated to Golden Rainbow.

Lou Anne Harrison Chessick organized a reunion party after the show with champagne and a buffet. When a few of us were overheard complaining about the price of the party ticket, our fabulous showgirl/ supporter Cindy Doumani simply wrote a check and paid for all the dancer/showgirls. What a classy lady.

While we were sitting out in the house as others rehearsed, Pam told me the greatest story:

Miss Bluebell always chartered a plane to ferry her dancers in and out of Las Vegas. Their visas were for only eighteen months at a time. On one return, Pam taxied to the airport with her friend Val. There, it was announced that the charter flight was delayed for one hour. Val called their stage manager Bill, with whom she had been having a steamy love affair, and announced that they had a surprise extra hour. Evidently, he said meet me at the Dunes and evidently she did so. In any case, she asked Pam to please see that her luggage got on the plane and told her that she was going to taxi back to the Dunes for a last fling with her sweetheart. Pam did so, then eventually boarded the plane with the thirty or so other girls, thinking that Val must be somewhere in the throng of performers. As the plane backed out and taxied slowly down the runway, Pam and the whole plane saw tall, blonde Val, in high heels, a full-length blonde mink coat and matching hat, sprinting down the runway, waving her arms overhead, yelling, "Stop! Stop!"

The pilot did stop, let down the stairs, and Val got on.

Both Pam and Val returned in another show, stayed, and both are still here in Las Vegas.

Chapter 39

Shecky

I took my two sons with me to see Shecky Greene at the Suncoast. He was here May 15, 16, and 17 of 2009. I went Sunday night. He was wonderful, as always, although he said, at eighty-three, he was a little tired from doing the Italian Earthquake Benefit at The Orleans that afternoon.

Nelson Sardelli organized the benefit. I understand it was very successful. Nelson is becoming well known for his expertise in that field. All the well-known comedians in town worked Nelson's Orleans benefit show, then came en mass to Shecky's Sunday night show at the Suncoast. One booth alone held David Brenner, Rich Little, Cork Proctor, Fielding West and The Great Tomasini, aka John Thompson, as well as Sardelli. Talk about supporting each other!

Each one graciously got up when called to the stage. Those men have been totally competitive with each other for years, but are now passionately supportive of each other. Generally, they regard Shecky as the champ, the best of the best, and Sheck had each one come on stage from the audience and do five or so minutes. It was a very special evening for the delighted and enthusiastic audience. Shecky Greene is truly synonymous with Las Vegas.

For me, it was wonderful to see Shecky looking all slender and healthy and in a good marriage at last. He was definitely "in voice," singing better than ever. Shecky and I dated for years, three or more. We both had other romantic interests, too, but we spent a lot of time together, mostly when he was here in Las Vegas at the Riviera lounge while I was a dancer in the showroom. That was my Merry Grass-Widow year, 1963.

I have many great memories of Sheck. Once, in Los Angeles, I was invited to accompany him to Rosh Hashana at Don Rickles' home. Earlier that evening, Shecky's mom taught me how to make potato pancakes — that is, she let me watch her do it! (It's best to drain them on a stack of newspapers covered with paper towels, then put them on a cookie sheet to keep them crisp in the oven.)

Another time in L.A., Shecky asked me to go with him to his ex-wife's house to pick up his two little daughters; one was three or so, the other a baby in wet diapers, changed by me, of course, in the car.

They were a handful, to say the least. It was obvious Sheck was heartbroken over losing his babies. But he had to take them back to their mother after supper, and he was on the road so much he didn't get to see them often. Allison, the baby, he hardly knew at all. My goodness, Dorie must be at least in her forties now.

In 1964, I joined *Bottoms Up*. Shecky came to see the show at the Castaways and I could hear him laugh at my little solo bit. I was especially tickled because I had written my own sketch. *Bottoms Up* then went on the road. I left the show for a while and did the never-opened show at the Aladdin, then went to Japan for the summer of 1965.

Home at the Playpen apartments again (a chic address for singles), I auditioned for the Jimmy Durante show again and went into rehearsal immediately. I remember that audition very well. I'd turned thirty-one on the plane to Japan, did a singing/dancing solo turn with great success in that show, and really thought I was hot stuff in the performing department. It was chilly the day of the audition, so I put on a full-length, white sheared-beaver coat over my black leotard audition outfit, swept onto the Desert Inn stage, glamorously tossed the coat on a convenient chair I'd spotted from the wings, and joined the lineup to audition for Ada Broadbent, Jimmy's longtime choreographer. I was a very different girl from the timid rube who arrived here ten years prior.

Jimmy's show was always a hugely successful run, with Sonny King as his sidekick and the incredible Jack Roth as his drummer. (A little sidebar here about Jack Roth: Because I'm a tap dancer, I recognize the importance of the drumbeat both in volume, time, and sound. Most of Jimmy's songs were in 2/4 time rather than 4/4, the more usual time signature. Two-four time, also called "Broadway two," takes more energy to drum, and Jimmy's style and charts took more energy to drum in general. So, Jack Roth, who was about Jimmy's age and had been with him as long as Eddie Jackson, had to work extra hard, and he did. His sound was incredible. The man beat those drums to death, two shows a night. He saved all his energy for the show, no hanging out backstage or socializing. I don't think I ever talked with him, but I loved his distinctive sound. It made me smile ear to ear. I think it was the main reason I so loved to work for Jimmy.)

The last week of the show, I heard that Jimmy was going to the Deauville Hotel in Miami Beach right after the Desert Inn engagement. I spoke to Ada immediately and asked if I could go with the show to Miami as I had a sister there I hadn't seen in ten years. She said no, it wouldn't work out, as she might have to change the choreography for the stage there, and the show opened the very next night, so there wasn't any time for rehearsal.

She was going ahead five or six days to audition and rehearse new girls. I also found out she was actually doing the same numbers and was really only talking about the few opening bars that might have to have a slight variation for the entrance. That annoyed me. She was breaking my heart because a change might possibly be a tiny little bit of trouble for her.

When we got to dress rehearsal on opening day, one of the Miami dancers showed me the entrance steps, and I did them instantly. Ada didn't have to do a thing.

After the Durante show (that was still in Las Vegas), I changed to street clothes and went to Jimmy's dressing room, knowing he would still be there getting his after-the-show massage. The door was still open, so I said, "Jimmy! Hello, hello, Jimmy, may I see you a moment?" He answered, "Come on in, sweetheart. Whata ya need?" (He called us all sweetheart) I asked him about Miami, adding, that, of course, I'd expect to pay my own airfare, and he immediately said, "Of course, you can go. Tell Ada I said so, no problem." Darling man!

Closing night at the Desert Inn, I brought my suitcases to work, joined the company leaving right after the last show and we all rode in the Desert Inn limos to the airport, where somebody checked in our luggage and put Jimmy, me, and two others of the company on a luggage cart and drove us across the tarmac to the stairs up to the plane.

Jimmy was too beloved and famous to board the usual way. People would mob him for autographs, might cause him to miss the plane. My sister picked me up in Miami with my nephews, and I was a happy lady.

Opening night at the Deauville Showroom was so much fun. Performing — singing, dancing, doing skits — was a joy for me. I also enjoyed meeting and getting to know the other Miami dancers. The last week of the engagement, one of the dancers mentioned that Shecky Greene was opening at the Fontainebleau Hotel that weekend, and that the Fontainebleau always had an opening night party to which other luminaries and all showdancers were invited.

Of course, I planned to go. I was going steady with the man I eventually married, but I also was still the playgirl of the Western World, and truth to tell, still carried a tiny little torch in my heart for Shecky. Three of the Durante dancers went with me. It was a lovely, crowded party, nice cheese and crackers and an open bar. Somebody, probably the entertainment director, was at the mic recognizing entertainers present, asking people to sing. A piano was handy and several accompanists on hand. Sheck was there when we arrived, surrounded by fans, friends, and several flirtatious girls. I caught his eye, but our glance turned into "Some Enchanted Evening"... across a crowed room. We hugged and lightly kissed showbiz-style, as the man at the mic called Shecky up to "say a few words. " Sheck removed his tie, unbuttoned his shirt, and headed for the mic, then turned and handed me his tie. I took that to mean, "You're my girl, wait here for me." After all, we had dated on and off for three years, never had a cross word. He did twenty hilarious minutes, then rejoined me.

The next morning, I woke up to find coffee already delivered by room service and the happy sound of Shecky singing in the shower. I opened the drapes to the brilliant Miami sunshine and thought *Oh no, horrors! I have nothing to wear! I'm going to have to walk across the elegant Fontainebleau lobby in my crumpled black satin evening suit with my black satin pumps at 11 a.m., surrounded by people in shorts and sandals.*

Dressed and sipping coffee, Shecky said, "Let's go out for breakfast," and I was forced to admit I would be embarrassed to death, I have nothing suitable to wear, so no breakfast for me, sob! He said he was going downstairs for a newspaper and would be right back and left. He returned twenty minutes later with a gorgeous blue silk shantung Capri set and Bernardo sandals to match. The lobby dress shop was open, he said. Would this do? I nearly died! It fit perfectly and was a favorite outfit for years. What a sweet, thoughtful thing to do, just so I wouldn't be embarrassed for a few minutes.

I went home to Las Vegas, rejoined *Bottoms Up* to perform a year at the Thunderbird. I married my son's father that year, 1966, and had son Ricky in 1967, working in the show until I was almost seven months along. Shecky came to see the show one afternoon, and we met in the bar afterward. I whispered in his ear, "Sheck, I have a secret! Wanna hear? I'm pregnant, due in July!" He turned and announced to the room, "Betty's going to have a baby!"

Along with half the world, I adore that man.

Shecky Greene

Chapter 40

Bottoms Up

When the entire Dick Humphries Dancers line was let go from the Riviera Hotel at the end of 1963, we all scrambled to find jobs, an inevitable on-going crisis in the dance business. We shared information about auditions and pending shows we'd heard about or at least I did. Our dear line-captain, Joyce Roberts, told me she had heard of a Texas show coming to town that was looking for an actress/singer/dancer.

"You do all that don't you, Betty? And you're from Texas!" she said. She handed me the phone number and man's name, Breck Wall, I'd never heard of him.

Next morning, I called the Houston number and told the voice that answered that I wanted to speak to Breck Wall please.

"This is Breck Wall," the voice gruffly said.

So I did my girl-looking-for-a-job-speech: Sir, My name is Betty Bunch, and I'm a dancer with extensive credits, and I'd like to audition for you if you'll tell me where and when you're holding auditions." I waited then for him to say something, but there was silence then a peculiar choking sound.

"Sir?" I said. Silence.

Finally the voice said, "Betty, honey, the job is yours if you want it.

This is Billy Ray. I changed my name to Breck Wall."

"Billy Ray Wilson who took me to the prom at the University of Texas in 1954? Are you still the best jitter-bug dancer in the world?" I asked. We were theatre majors. Show biz is a small world. I nearly died.

We arranged for me to fly to Houston to join the company and learn the show before it opened at the Castaways on the Strip in May 1964. The Castaways was a little north of Spring Mountain Road, across from the Desert Inn just south of the New Frontier. All these places are gone now. Sob.

When I arrived in Houston three days later it was cold and windy, in April. I wore my elegant cream wool boucle Lilly Ann suit with cream fox collar and cuffs, black cashmere sweater with pearls, real of course, black leather Andrew Geller pumps and handbag from Joseph Magnin. J.Magnin was in a free standing building next to the Desert Inn. I was sporting my curly baby doll haircut, the latest thing, and long red nails, also real. I never ever wore fake nails. Tacky.

Breck met me at the bottom of the stairs off the plane at Houston International. I couldn't believe my eyes: pimples all gone, four rubber band braces all gone, a tall and handsome young man now. We hugged and whooped Texas style. Then showing me a little of the new-to-me "boss" style, he said, "Don't ever call me Billy Ray again. I mean it."

The show was playing the Continental Hotel in downtown Houston to great reviews and full houses. Breck carried my luggage and checked me into my complementary room, made plans to meet me for dinner in the hotel coffee shop and then to see the 8 p.m. show.

Breck and his partner in life and business, Joe Peterson, sat with me ringside. Breck wasn't really in the show in those days. He did the opening and the finale so as to make the company look bigger, but didn't do any lines or solos. I laughed myself silly. It was a really cute, fresh college-style show, only very slightly risqué. Breck had not yet become a dirty old man. It was loosely based on the style of Ken Murray's *Blackouts*, and/or *Hellzapoppin'*, both big hits on Broadway in the forties. The stars of the show were the adorable 300 pound Kewpie Doll, Nancy Austin, and the great Bill Fanning, who morphed from line-backer to fey in the blink of an eye.

I stayed with *Bottoms Up* for the next six years, left three or four times, but always came back when asked. After six months at the Castaways to great acclaim, we went to San Francisco, where I left after a fight with Breck, but returned to do a full year at the old Thunderbird which had a little jewel of a showroom, then I left again to have a baby having married early that run, then returned for a long run, over a year at Caesars Palace.

Bottoms Up was a family. We even dressed together all in one room, laughing and telling all about our day since we parted twelve hours before. Breck threw big cake parties on our birthdays, and we exchanged expensive gifts like brothers and sisters. We kept up with news of the nation, too, which led to timely comments during the show.

One year we did *Everything Lyndon Does is for the Birds*. I sang the Lady Bird role.

Nancy was always under orders from her doctor to lose weight. When we were at Caesars Palace, the House Doctor, Dr. Fink, often came backstage to take her blood pressure, then always announced he wasn't going to allow her to perform because her blood pressure was too high.

Nancy then called him Doctor Quack, said she felt fine, and did the show as usual. We all sat together in the coffee shop between shows. After Nancy finished her small salad, she went around the table saying, "Did you want me to have that piece of toast? Did you want me to have a bite of that pie?" She was hilarious.

Learning the show in Houston, I quickly found out there was no rest for the weary after the show. Breck considered one hour plenty of time to catch your breath and get a snack before the game of the day began. In Houston, it was Scrabble, usually played in Breck's room with four or five of us piled on the bed, board in the middle. We played for blood. Breck was the most serious game player in the world with screaming threats and laughter until we choked. We often played until sunrise. Over the years we got tired of Scrabble and played charades for a couple of years.

We were fiercely competitive, playing the team version. Breck was always one of the captains and always choose me first. Our team always won, if we didn't, Breck had a tantrum and demanded a rematch until we did win. At the Castaways, Redd Fox was also appearing and alternated with us. One night he joined us after the last show, but said he didn't know how to play. Guess who was delegated to teach him? I was happy to do that, He was so good natured and overwhelmed with our over-the-top antics. What a nice man.

Breck worked like a demon. When we closed a venue, he sent the company home to pack and get some rest while he packed the entire show, props, costumes, wigs, everything into big cartons. When we arrived at the new dressing room in the new city, there were our names posted on the mirrors, every detail in place. Opening costumes hung right behind our chairs, second costumes right next to it, and so on; shoes lined up under the appropriate costume, even the show jewelry was carefully placed at the proper performers place. We were well known for our lightning fast changes, accomplished because we girls wore flesh-colored bikinis, custom made for each of us. We could take off a costume and put on another while standing in the wings.

I loved doing the actual work — dancing, sketch comedy, and singing comedy numbers. One of my proudest claims in a long career is that when I finally left the show for good, it took two new performers to cover my part. *Bottoms Up* played three years on the Las Vegas Strip doing capacity business, first at the Castaways for six months, then at the old Thunderbird for more than a year and then at Caesars Palace for more than a year.

The show went on without me for another thirty-five years, getting dirtier and dirtier as it went along. New Year's Eve, 1968, we dressed for the 2 p.m. show, then someone checked the house and discovered no one was there! Breck went out to investigate and returned to tell us management forgot to mention that show was canceled because Evel Knievel was jumping the fountains. We threw on our jeans, and watched the whole thing from the Caesars Palace front steps along with thousands of other folks. It was awful to watch him bounce knowing he was breaking bones.

It was a fabulous three years on the Strip and three years on the road. We were invited everywhere, introduced everywhere, in the Las Vegas Review-Journal every day. We were stars! Yes, I miss it so much, and miss my old *Bottoms Up* family so much. It was a smash hit, very funny and different from anything that had ever played the Strip. Of course entertainment professionals recognized the format as the same as *Hellzapoppin'* and *Blackouts*. Real historians no doubt saw the resemblance to early burlesque when it first evolved from Vaudeville. The format was simply song and dance numbers interspersed with sketch comedy. After the punchline, there was a blackout with a musical vamp until the next number, maybe another sketch, maybe a musical number.

It was mildly suggestive, milk toast compared to today's shows. You could call it "corny" or you could call it "timeless and classic." Forrest Duke loved it! Ralph Pearl loved it! All crictics loved it. We pretty soon were playing to full houses, everybody came to see us.

We were loved! We had fans!

We opened May 1964 during the coolest May anybody could remember. I had told the other girls in Houston that it would be 100 degrees or more, so they only brought summer clothes and were freezing. I took them to my apartment and handed out jackets and long-sleeved blouses and dresses. I've always been a clotheshorse, so I had a huge closet full, and anyway they wanted to see my apartment. Susie, from Dallas, was to room with me. It was a big two bedroom place just off the pool on Lynnwood Street, off Sahara Avenue just southeast of the Strip. My roommate Maureen (Moe) from the Riviera was returning to England.

After our last dress rehearsal, I invited Nancy Austin, our star, and her comedy partner to come over for dinner with Susie and me. I stopped at the grocery on the way home, and in one hour flat, had a Southern fried chicken dinner on the table, mashed potatoes and gravy, green salad, and "bought " pie with ice cream. They were impressed to no end. I was always a housewife at heart and had Revere Ware, china and silver up the ying-yang. And, I'm a show-off then and here! Heck, it's better than being a slob.

After six hugely successful months at the Castaways, we closed, and we were booked into a nightclub in North Beach in San Francisco. Breck told me the salary and I said, sorry, I can't go, it's too little to pay my rent here and there, too, even rooming with another girl from the show. Mine was a nice apartment all set up and I didn't want to store my tons of stuff. This made Breck and Joe (Breck's partner) furious.

Finally, I said OK, I'd come if he could arrange to squeeze out just another $25 when he got to San Francisco. Then, I wouldn't make any money, but wouldn't go in the hole either. Two days later, he had Jan (our dumb blond character) call me to say Breck told her to tell me to come on up, yes, he'd fixed the money thing, and just didn't have time to call himself.

So I booked the next flight to San Francisco, taxied as instructed to the North Beach club and innocently joined the rehearsal. I found out to my horror that the other three girls had found an apartment (prescouted by Breck) with room for three, but not four in a second class (really third-class) hotel, they didn't know whether or not a single was available there, and if I didn't stay with them, I'd have to taxi to work and back alone every night. To make a long story short, the hotel, really a rooming house, did have one single on the ground floor. I said I'll take it without even looking. What choice did I have? The room was unbelievable: linoleum floor, one cast-iron twin bed with bare springs and a three-inch mattress, no linens. One electrical wire hanging center room with a bare light bulb. One very small cardboard chest of drawers. Large bath containing another bare light blub, but, the only saving grace, a huge old clawfoot tub with a rubber stopper and a soap-cage hanging on the rim. I asked where the linens were and was told there was a Woolworth's across the street where I could buy a pillow, towels, blanket, and sheets. Worse of all, there was a window, almost stuck shut, but you could see, barely, the ground through the dirty glass and tan paper pull-down shade. It felt decidedly unsafe. The other girls, feeling sorry for me, said I could watch TV at their place if I liked. They were two floors up.

Fortunately, I had on impulse packed a thick anthology of poetry, my only entertainment. I discovered at the club the next night that Breck wasn't speaking to me. On payday night, I found out why: the amount was the same as the amount I said I couldn't work for. He'd had Jan lie to me.

My best quality is making the best of things when there is no recourse. So I set about seeing San Francisco. A trolley line went right in front of my dump, and wonder of wonders, there was a great bakery with great French pastries and coffee right next door. Later, I discovered a fabulous Hungarian goulash place just two blocks away, and a tiny grocery for peanut-butter, crackers, and fruit.

Then one night at the North Beach bar, I met a tall, charming, educated fellow who starting taking me out to dinner at some of San Francisco's finer places. He turned out to be a state Legislator from Napa Valley, and he proceeded to teach me all about California wines on my one night off per week, and we sometimes went out for a fast supper between shows.

He was a doll. He announced casually that he had a small yacht out in the bay, would I like to go for a cruise on Sunday, my day off. Would I! He said to dress warmly. He picked me up at 9 a.m. and we drove in his little black Jaguar to the Yacht Club on the Bay.

He hadn't mentioned it before, but it was actually, he said, the San Francisco Yacht Club's annual Regatta. Further, it was a serious race he wanted to win, so he had hired a professional captain, who told me I had a very important job, to be ballast, and I must jump to the other side of the boat when told to do so. During the race he yelled "Coming about! Betty, Jump!"

The boat was an Ariel class, which means it was 34-feet long. My date informed me we'd probably spend most of our time in the water running on the edge of the boat, which is exactly what we did. There was a ledge, actually the benchseat, for me to stand on and when I looked down at my feet, they were only a very short distance, maybe twelve inches, above the water. The bay was choppy. The course was around Alcatraz and back to the departure line. To say I was scared is the understatement of the year. I was terrified and frozen.

Yacht racing is just a big game of chicken. No kidding. Since the larger boat has the right of way, it's critical for the captain with his bull horn, to know the exact sizes of various boats at a glance so he can yell, "Give Way, Give Way!" If the other boat is even one foot longer, it has the right of way, so then the captain tries to bluff.

The upshot is that two or more boats are running on a direct collision course and the more reckless one wins by refusing to pull up until the very last minute. Or not.

Guess what. We won that race. My name was listed as "crew" in the paper the next day, and my date got a big silver trophy. We spent the evening drinking at the bar of the yacht club, and being bought drinks and congratulated. So Bryce (I've finally remembered his name) and I never got past the kiss goodnight stage. It's just as well since I consider that I've been sailing twice. First time and last time.

Bottoms Up was held over four weeks, but I gave Breck my two-week notice as I was tired of his not speaking to me and being a jerk. I've already told you about then getting the very prestigious job at the Aladdin, the show that never opened, and then going to Japan for the entire summer. When I got back, Breck came over to see me, we made up, and he asked me to come back to the show and said that we had a great booking at the Thunderbird Hotel, probably for a year. And it was. What a year! Nothing is as fun as being in a hit show. Breck kept an ad in the *Las Vegas Review-Journal* every day with our pictures and names, so everybody knew who we were.

We were invited to openings often, and we could go since we only played afternoons.

One time I heard someone stage-whisper, "That's Betty Bunch," as I walked by. Talk about thrilled. I floated.

Another evening, a lovely young black girl stopped me. "Aren't you from *Bottoms Up*? Betty, right?" she said, shaking my hand. "I'm Tina Turner, love your performance." She and her husband, Ike, played the lounge at the International Hotel, now the Hilton. We chatted awhile. She was so lovely and charming. Over the years, I've been so glad for her huge success.

Everybody came to see us. One afternoon the house booth held Dan Rowen and Dick Martin. A few days later, they came back and brought Johnny Carson. Not incidentally, he owned part of CBS. A few months later, we turned on the television to watch a heavily advertised new show, Laugh In. It was a slightly altered Bottoms Up. We were heartsick, or at least I was. Coulda, shoulda, woulda.

Also that year, I fell in love with the boy next door. We drove up to Tonopah, Nevada, on our one day off, and got married. The bride wore lavender matching jeans and jacket; the groom wore cowboy boots and hat with his jeans. A Tonopah judge did the ceremony. It was a beautiful, sincere, lovely service, to my surprise. I started right away trying to get pregnant, succeeded three months later.

Breck wouldn't hear of my leaving the show, so I danced and worked until I was almost seven months along. One Tuesday after our day off, I came into the dressing room, put on the opening costume, looked in the mirror, and wailed, "Breck! Breck! I can't do the show! Look at me!" I had popped out over night, a common phenomenon.

Breck insisted I didn't look all that bad, and that he wanted me to work two more days. That turned out to be to give him time to plan a party for me after my last show two nights later. It was so sweet, a real surprise, with cake, Champagne and a beautiful gold charm from the cast, a baby on a coin with its bottom sticking out the other side, engraved to Beulah (my company name.) Breck even had my husband, Joel, there. I cried, of course. The girls had already given me a shower at Breck's beautiful home on the golf course. I cried even harder in the car on the way home.

Carick Alan (Rick) Rosenthal was born July 1, 1967, at Sunrise Hospital on Maryland Parkway. March 1968, I was back in the show for a year's run at Caesars Palace. But that's another story.

with Breck Wall

DAVID HARRIS
Another Dallasite, David Harris, rejoins Bottoms Up for the first time in six years. Part of that time was spent in the U.S. Army as an M.P. He has since traveled the Playboy Clubs in his own revue "Get The Girl" and "Sex and the Single Boy" for two years.

ROB BARRON
This handsome lad is beginning his third year with Bottoms Up. Last year he won Bravo's for his excellent performance in the Thunderbirds production of "That Certain Girl" opposite Virginia Mayo, Walter Slezak, and Dennis O'Keefe. He is married to feature dancer Marina Manbert.

BETTY BUNCH
An accomplished actress as well as a talented dancer, Betty Bunch has appeared in motion pictures South Pacific, Jeanne Eagels and My Fair Lady. She recently married local real estate broker Joel Rosenthal.

JAN SUTTON
A former Miss Texas and one of Dallas' leading fashion models, Jan Sutton has often appeared in Mademoiselle and Harper's Bazaar. With the Texas Rangerettes at the Riviera Hotel she performed with such stars as Liberace, Eddie Fisher and Nancy Wilson. The last seven productions of Bottoms Up have featured Miss Sutton.

MARY ANN BRADLEY
This petite young lassie has been seen in many Las Vegas productions at the Sahara, Riviera and Aladdin Hotels. Mary Ann Bradley begins her second year with Bottoms Up and is married to the very popular Dave Bradley, head of Public Relations for the Sahara Hotel.

JOYCE GREENWOOD
This exciting performer is from Garland, Texas, and last year was featured dancer in "La Dolce Mini-Girls" at the Riviera Hotel. Joyce Greenwood also toured in the National Company of "Funny Girl" before coming to Vegas.

BETTINA BRENNA
This tall (6'4") knockout will soon be seen in the motion picture "Funny Girl" and will be in the coming edition of Playboy with the very sexy Woody Allen. Bettina Brenna is the newest member of Bottoms Up having just completed "It's Hell" at the Frontier Hotel.

JOE PETERSON, co-producer
Mr. Peterson is the essential man-behind-the-scene responsible for the design and execution of costumes and scenery and for the writing of several numbers in the show. He and Breck Wall first produced Bottoms Up in Dallas, later opening The Playbill, a club which helped develop many revue personalities. Since then they've taken Bottoms Up to Houston, Las Vegas, Lake Tahoe, Honolulu, Reno, and Tucson.

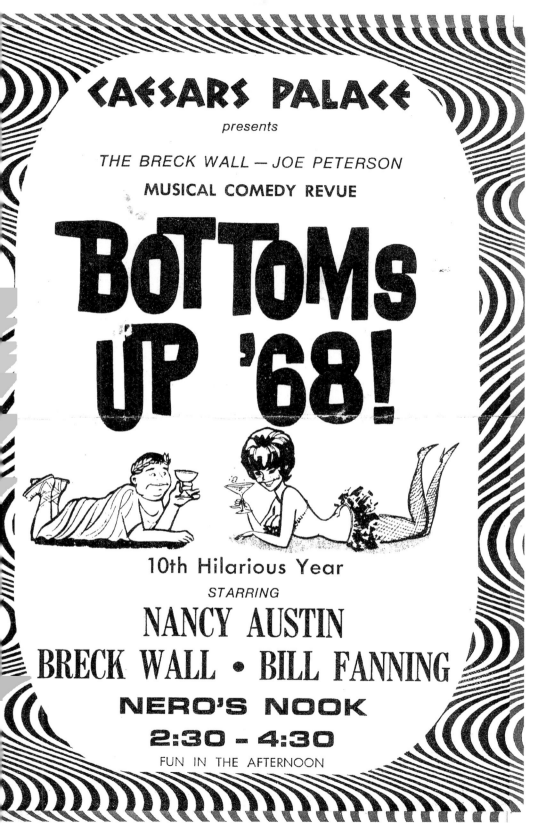

Chapter 41

Breck Wall

*I*f I'm going to write a story about Breck Wall's life, and death five days short of his seventh-six birthday, I should start off with "Goodnight Sweet Prince." since we studied Shakespeare at the University of Texas in 1954 and cliques are good.

But I'm sure Breck would insist that I change it to "Goodnight Sweet Queen," so consider it done Billy Ray.

And he would also threaten to put me on the shit list for using the name he so detested. The shit list was a real punishment from the boss and it meant he didn't speak to you for an extended length of time, and frowned at anyone who did. It was not fun.

He didn't really hate his name, just what it represented. And what it represented, his life as a little boy, would bring tears to your eyes. Billy Ray's parents were alcoholics. He didn't remember what his mother looked like, he told me, because she was always passed out on the couch. She died when he was five or six.

His father married another alcoholic woman he met at the local bar, who, of course, had little interest in her new step-son.

Billy Ray learned to forage for himself in the kitchen, seldom getting a real meal, unless he was invited to supper at his playmates house down the street.

When he turned ten or so, he packed a small suitcase, walked to his friend's house, and was found sitting on the front steps waiting for his friend's mother. She became his stepmother after he told her he was never going back there and asked if he could stay with her. Nonie took him in, taught him many things, saw him through high school, and helped him find a part-time job at J.C. Penny's haberdashery department. She taught him how to save his money and budget so he could go to the university, where I met him. Further, he was badly dyslexic and had to work hard to get passing grades.

One of the things Nonie taught him that always impressed me no end was to make his bed first thing in the morning. Bottom's Up cast members often stayed together in rented houses or motels. I've seen Breck get up in the morning, get his feet on the floor, turn around and make up the bed before he even went to the bathroom. He did that every day without fail.

Breck simply worked harder than anyone I ever met. So, I think he deserved his success despite the truth: that he stole most of the material and comedy ideas in the show. He went to New York every year to scout the off-Broadway shows for material and managed to steal it. I don't know how, tape recorder? David Harris, Suzanne Buhrer, and Bill Fanning constantly wrote or spoke material that Breck simply appropriated with no talk of credit or money.

Breck was a ball of energy and enthusiasm and tons of fun. He never sulked, whatever he didn't like, everyone knew about it right away. You never had to wonder about what the boss thought of you, he expressed it instantly. He started every conversation with an insult. Older ladies, like my Mother, got, "Hello, you old bag."

When we made the move from Houston to Las Vegas, I learned another aspect of Breck's character. He organized that trip within an inch of its life. The cast had, as I remember, four cars between us. Breck dictated whose car you were to go in, and how long you could drive before he stopped the caravan and shifted riders and drivers around so nobody got tired at the wheel, or bored with their seatmates. And he had packed up the entire show personally, earrings, gloves, props, all labeled and neatly placed in cartons. He never overlooked a single detail. Brecky was a Mother Hen, flapping his wings, clucking and bustling all over, protecting his flock, herding his baby chicks and checking the eggs, too. He gave a vicious peck to anything or anybody who got in his way.

He gave all the girls nicknames. Mine was Beulah. The gorgeous Jan Sutton was Buttons or Button-Sutton for reasons we only found out in the dressing room. Nancy Austin was always Nanny.

Breck's fatal flaw was, of course, his ego. He couldn't bear to be treated as anything less than royalty. For years after I left the show, I was still considered *Bottoms Up* family and always visited the dressing room. Once, Breck dressed hurriedly and left. I stayed to visit David and Motts, and casually asked where Breck was going. They told me there was a big party the cast had been invited to, but Breck hadn't mentioned it to them, so they weren't going. The boss preferred to collect accolades alone. Evidently Breck didn't realize they had been invited just as he was. They told me he often did that, show openings and things they'd love to have done.

Same big problem way back at Caesars Palace when we were such a huge success in 1964, had major consequences. At the end of a year when he and Joe had "poor-mouthed" all year, saying they couldn't afford to pay rehearsal pay, or give raises commensurate with our success, they bought a big gorgeous home on the golf course, bought each other very expensive Christmas gifts (huge color TV, mink lined jackets) and gave lavish parties.

Nancy was clearly the star of the show and demanded a raise. They refused, Nancy left, and the show was never as good again. Or at least that's my opinion. *Laugh In* was a huge hit on television and it coulda, shoulda, woulda been us if Breck and Joe had been on the ball. Nancy, so talented, was reduced to *Sex over Forty* at the Continental Hotel. They needed each other.

May you rest in peace Billy Ray Wilson. With no help from anyone, and against all odds, you turned yourself into a star, Breck Wall. So I don't care what anyone thinks, what the newspapers have written, or what everybody knows, I like you.

Hell, I loved you.....Beulah

I've already told you a lot about my years in *Bottoms Up*, but I don't feel I've really conveyed the kooky and singular character of my cast mates.

Jan Sutton from Dallas was gorgeous. She did lots of modeling (Dallas is a big fashion center) and loved dancing, too. But it was her personality that made her one of a kind — that and her voice. Newspaper critics of the time likened it to a rusty gate. And, of course, there was her Texas accent.

Jan had two babies, who were always with us. She'd had one at fifteen, Bobby, and Jana was born when Jan was seventeen.

Both Breck Wall and his partner, Joe, were in love with Jan. Most men fell in love with her at first glance. Breck promised her that he would always help take care of the babies if she would join *Bottoms Up* on the road, meaning Houston at the time. The show played Dallas at the Adolphus Hotel with huge success for two years, I think it was, before it was finally time to go elsewhere, so Breck found a great agent, Larry Gragson, packed it up and they went to Houston.

After my opening night in the show in Houston, I went with Jan up to our complimentary hotel rooms. Hers was next to mine, so I went in with her to check on the children, who were supposed to be asleep. Bobby was, but Jana had found Mommy's lipsticks in the bath and drew all over the big mirror in several shades and included part of the wall next to the mirror.

Jan kept cleaning supplies in the room, and with a little help from me, we had it cleaned up pretty quickly because Breck kept calling to say, 'Hurry up, we've started playing (we played Scrabble every night after the show). Jan was allowed off only if a baby was sick. Then, of course, she had to spend time lecturing Jana about the importance of not making a mess in the nice rooms.

Larry Gragson next booked us into Las Vegas at the Castaways, then three months on the road, then, at last, back in Las Vegas at the Thunderbird for a year and finally afternoons at Caesars Palace, where we were in high cotton. It was at Caesars that Jan took up knitting. She wanted to quit smoking and thought knitting would keep her hands busy. She learned knit one, pearl two, had someone cast on as wide as the needles would allow and knitted for the next two years.

David Harris kept asking her what it was going to be, and she always said, "You'll find out when I finish." She had chosen yellow yarn, but when she ran out of it, she just bought another shade of yellow. Further, it had been dragged all over and was filthy on the end. At the 20-foot mark, she got someone to take it off the needles for her and took it to be dry-cleaned. She folded it and put it in a tissue-lined Neiman Marcus box and presented it to Breck for Christmas, elaborately wrapped and bowed.

In the meantime the cast had gotten into joke cakes in general. For his birthday, David Harris gave Breck a football cake, since Breck was a football fanatic. However, it was a real football, frosted by David, so when Breck tried to cut it, the knife wouldn't dent it.

A little aside here ... the year the Texas Longhorns played in the

Rose Bowl, Breck chartered a two-passenger plane, invited me to go along and we screamed ourselves silly, barely made it back to Las Vegas on time to do the show at Caesars. We could hardly speak, much less sing and project. Breck did things like that. The pilot thought we were crazy. I wonder why.

The scarf saga went on and on for years. Someone carefully wrapped it in Saran Wrap and frosted it in chocolate, and someone put it in a large mailing tube.

Jan got married one year and mentioned to David that she wanted a large, framed picture of some kind to go over the fireplace in her new home she was so carefully decorating. That year for her birthday, he gave her a beautiful, wood-carved, large, impressive frame. Jan loved it and had a fit over it. David explained that the canvas was in the car. He hadn't had time to mount it in the frame. It was the scarf, carefully and artistically swirled over the canvas, held with push-pins. Unfortunately, it had gotten dirty again over the years and had little dots of chocolate frosting here and there. I think that's when Jan decided to retire the thing.

Breck got dirtier and dirtier after Caesars, and I was long gone to have babies. The show went to Australia for almost a year without me. Breck found somewhere a small plaster penis, gilded gold. He called it the golden cock, and he presented it to anybody who made a little mistake that show.

Bill Fanning was one of the funniest people around. When he arrived at a party (we had lots of those), he paused in the doorway long enough to have everyone's attention, then loudly said, "Where's the john?"

My personal schtick, arriving at a party, was to do a cartwheel, high heels and all, into the center of the room.

Ah, the excesses of youth. Did I love being in that show!

with Breck Wall

Chapter 42

C.A. "Rick" Rosenthal Weighs In

I like to think I'm the product of a typical Las Vegas story. My mother, Betty Bunch, moved to Las Vegas in 1956 to perform as a dancer on the Strip. She was a Moro-Landis Dancer in the Donald O'Connor Show at the Sahara. Twelve years and five or six hotels later, still dancing on the Strip, she opened as a principal and dancer in the original production of *Bottoms Up* starring Nancy Austin, at Caesars Palace where they stayed for a year. While she was pregnant with me, we did two shows a day at the Thunderbird Hotel, also in *Bottoms Up*.

She continued to perform on the Strip until my brother Dan was born in 1970. He did two shows per day with her in *Once Upon A Mattress* at the Desert Inn. She sang the role of the Queen.

My father, Joel Rosenthal, moved here in 1960. His story is equally unique to Las Vegas. He and a friend saw an ad in the *Chicago Tribune* offering a job to drive a new Cadillac from Chicago to Las Vegas in return for a small stipend and a free train ticket home. Being twenty-one and recently discharged from the Army, this turned out to be a great adventure for both of them.

After arriving in Vegas and spending the weekend, my father announced to his friend that he wasn't going back to Chicago. He wanted to stay and make Las Vegas his home, so that's exactly what he did. My father's first job was shilling 21 at the Las Vegas Club for $1 an hour. He thought he'd died and gone to heaven.

Needless to say, his parents were not thrilled and came west by train to take him home. They weren't successful. Jackie Gaughan sent him down to the basement to learn to deal craps and eventually put him on the game. He lived and worked here in Las Vegas from 1960 until his death in 1996. During that time he worked as a dealer and then floorman at Binion's Horseshoe, the Tropicana, and the Desert Inn. Then in 1968, he became a real estate broker and developer. He and Mom built the first handicapped-accessible apartments in the state, behind Southern Memorial Hospital.

In 1979 my father was appointed to the post of public administrator. A year later, he won the 1980 election for the post by a landslide, receiving more votes than any other local Democratic office-seeker during that year's heavily-favored Republican sweep, the Reagan Revolution as it's come to be called.

My father had a real estate office, Rosenthal Realty, in the Valley Bank Plaza and kept the same post office box, No. 673, downtown for all thirty-six years of his residency here.

Meanwhile Mom became a cookie-baking, stay-at-home mother, was president of Twin Lakes Elementary School PTA, lobbied in Carson City for the PTA earning a State Life PTA pin, served the March of Dimes, worked on Governor Richard Bryan's and others' political campaigns, and went back to school to earn a bachelor's degree in American studies from University of Nevada, Las Vegas. She had left the University of Texas lacking eighteen hours on a theater degree and always was determined to get a bachelor's degree. She later participated in UNLV's living history program as one of the women who made Las Vegas what it is today.

My brother and I went to Twin Lakes Elementary School, Gibson Middle School, Western High School, and UNLV. My brother Dan Rosenthal's degree is in hotel administration, my degree is in recreation. I've worked for the city of Las Vegas Leisure Services Department since 1989 and feel very fortunate to have grown up here. My family and I love Las Vegas for what it was and for what it has become.

Back to Betty

I'll be attending the Old Timer's Reunion at The Orleans soon and thought these remembrances by my son, written for the Las Vegas Centennial, were appropriate for my readers to hear. Further, I'm writing this story on October 15, 2008, and the Las Vegas Review-Journal headline is "Frank (Lefty) Rosenthal dead at 79."

Oh the grief that man caused my family! One day my two boys came home from Twin Lakes almost in tears. They came in the kitchen and said, "Mommy, is our Daddy a criminal? Kids at school said our Daddy is a thief and a murderer. Is he?" Of course I explained at length and in detail, but they were still upset. Children are so cruel to each other. We were the only other Rosenthal's in town then and Lefty's wife was an ex-showgirl, too.

We lived in a wonderful neighborhood, Stonehaven, across from the municipal golf course, where we could hear Siegfried and Roy's tigers roar every morning for food and every evening as they were loaded into the truck to go to work. We all saw them first at the Frontier then at the Stardust, and loved them. It was so fun to see that act grow over the years. They lived just down the street. At Halloween, the line of children in costume was two blocks long as Siegfried and Roy had a reputation for generosity. One year they gave each child one of those giant Hersey one-pound bars. Another year it was a brown paper lunch sack full of goodies tied with ribbon. One year it was a silver dollar each!

It was kind of a rural area. Texas Station was years away as was Summerlin. A girlfriend of mine, Tracy, a Bluebell (English dancer) lived a block away and kept goats and chickens, a lovely garden and, believe it or not, a bee hive with fresh honey! I'm still grateful to her for teaching my boys proper English table manners as they played with her boys. She and I and Linda Atchley fed whosever children were around. Tony Atchley, legendary publicity man, and his family lived across the street. Their son Mike went on to become a fireman, I believe. Lovely people. Lots of Mormon neighbors there. When Karen Barfield brought over fresh-baked Mormon whole wheat bread made from freshly ground wheat, it eclipsed whatever I made for dinner. What a joy.

I had a big prolific fig tree and put up fig jam every morning in July. On the Fourth of July we had a block party, all the children playing fireworks with their fathers. And another block party on Halloween. Some of us carried cocktails around to sip out on the sidewalk while watching our little ones, to be replenished by friendly neighbors as we went along.

All the neighborhood children, especially the boys of course, lived summers in the desert nearby, catching lizards, running barefoot half the time, to my terror. We had Bag Balm on hand for nightly application to their little feet.

Melody Lane ran behind our house and folks there still had horses. We all secretly kept desert tortoises in our backyards. You weren't supposed to capture them, they were endangered, but we all saved them from certain death in the roadway. I picked up our first one on Decatur at Sahara in front of Wonderworld, which was on the northeast corner where Vons is now. Decatur, a two-lane highway, was the end of town, it was all desert on the west side. The giant twelve-inch by fourteen-inch tortoise was headed north on the yellow line and would have been killed I was sure. Redneck cowboys liked to run over them with their pickups. Eventually, we had thirty-six, a whole colony. Discovering tiny two-inch baby tortoises bravely marching around the back yard was an occasion for yelps and screams every spring. If you want one today, you can visit tortoisegroup.org and learn more about adopting a tortoise.

Bike riding was the main children's activity in Stonehaven. My two boys discovered the Las Vegas Wash and its cement culvert snaking toward downtown. They learned to throw their bikes over the chain-link fence, climb over and retrieve the bikes, then ride up and down the sides. Of course, we had no idea. Once, Danny and his buddy inadvertently found themselves on the freeway, had no idea how they'd gotten there from the culvert, but just kept riding along until the Nevada Highway Patrol stopped them, and called Joel to come get them. He was on the scene of a death as public administrator so the officer ended up bringing them home, bikes sticking out of the trunk, riding happily in the front seat. We were still a small town then.

I was able to stay home and take care of my family for ten years. Halcyon days for me. Wish I had some of that fig jam on Mormon home-baked bread.

with my sons Carick "Rick" (left) and Dan Rosenthal (right)

Chapter 43

The Last Dance

*I*t was the best of times, it was the worst of times. Tears mixed with laughter, old mixed with young, ecstatic talked to depressed, all united by a common background of working at the Tropicana in the *Folies Bergere*. No other show in Las Vegas had run for forty-nine years. *Jubilee!* is close at more than forty years.

The last dance at the *Folies Bergere* at the Tropicana Hotel on the Strip in Las Vegas was performed for invited guests, nearly all alumni, on March 28, 2009. The last curtain fell at 9:35 p.m. It was wonderful, wild and wacky, wistful and woeful. It was also gawdawful for the 600 or so alumni of the forty-nine-year-old show to sit there and watch the death of an old friend while cheering, applauding, and pretending all was well. The death rattle was only a little muffled by cake and champagne.

The best of times was seeing friends you hadn't seen in forever, noticing how terrific or how old they looked. Most looked fabulous, show people work at that. The worse was realizing you were again seeing the last of an era, something grand, now gone, never to be again. Part of the grief was coming face to face with the abuse and neglect from the corporate side of the hotel. One of our most gifted director choreographers was simply not given the means to keep refurbishing the elderly costumes, the worn out sets, the fabulous but getting-tired definitive headpieces worn by the famous topless showgirls. Only a director of the superior caliber of Jerry Jackson could, despite such problems, present a beautiful show, showcasing top-level dancers at the top of their form and beautiful women at the top of theirs.

I hadn't seen the show in years, but well remember the different levels of the sets, gone except for the cancan number. The lavish costumes, also for the most part were gone except for the cancan, and maybe some of the opening. The Rudas Australian acrobatic dancers, gone, replaced in part by other dancer acrobats, mostly men. Jerry's elaborate dance steps turned the *Folies* into a dance show, rather than a spectacle. That was fine with me, but perhaps not as advertised. The hotel evidently didn't care.

The cancan finale was the most famous number in the *Folies*, and the element and dance most closely associated with French shows. The one at the *Folies* was outstanding of its genre. However, I, and most of the dancers I know or have ever known, loathe, hate, despise, dread and disparage the cancan. It's the most brutal of cliché dance numbers. The skirt is always incredibly heavy, fifteen pounds or so would be common. You never stop jumping up and down hauling that skirt from side to side and kicking over the head, and the dang thing always ends in a spine-jarring jump-split, painful but welcome because now at least it's over until the next show and for the moment you can breathe again. All of that is good reason to dislike that dance, but why the hate?

Because many dancers have studied history of dance and therefore know that the cancan was considered naughty and vulgar back in the 1890s, and it was, because women of the time didn't wear underpants. Got it? Gives *Ta-ra-ra Boom-de-ay* a whole new meaning, huh?

Meanwhile I personally had a great time. I was given my first press pass, a big deal to me, and was escorted past the waiting admission line to a cordoned off area full of professional cameras, and real reporters using laptops and looking serious.

Then came my big thrill for the night: I had looked forward to visiting with Jerry Jackson, who was a dear friend fifty-one years before but whom I hadn't seen since. When my year at the Sahara, 1956, was over, I called and got an audition time to meet Donn Arden, but when I got to the Desert Inn Showroom, it was Jerry Jackson working for Donn, who met me at the door, took me up on stage, and actually gave me the dance audition. I was of course scared, but Jerry was so dear, relaxed, and kind, that I did fine and was invited to move to Hollywood and work for Donn. Jerry was in the show at the Moulin Rouge in Hollywood, too, so we always chatted backstage and I considered him a supportive friend. There's lots of jealousy and bitchiness in show business, so you have to kind of watch with whom you share confidences. Jerry was safe. At the *Folies* last performance, I was delighted to look up and see him being interviewed on camera in the press area not ten feet away from me. When the interview was over, I bolted to his side, got a big hug, an OMG and a picture.

My pal Renee De Haven, wearing a beautiful pink sport coat, sat with me. We had a great time dishing and saying, "Oh look, there's whoever."

Renee is another choreographer who danced in the line with me back in 1957, '58, and '59 and is still a friend. Believe it or not, he is eighty-eight and still choreographs shows around town, amazing. But I see Renee often.

Also gracing the room was Jim Hodge who was the production singer for every French show in town, as was Carl Lindstrom attending with his dancer wife, Henrietta.

Forever beautiful, showgirls and friends of mine in attendance included Margie Fields, Joni Saylon, Ellie Swarie, Lisa Metford, Jeanie Stevens, and Renee Lee. Grace Meoli looks exactly the same as she did thirty-eight years ago when she and I were in *Bottoms Up* at Caesars Palace. Fred Doumani told me when he and his brother owned the hotel (in the early seventies), the show was lots bigger. It was nice to see gentleman producer Maynard Sloat looking so well and spiffy. He must be winning at Del Mar. Cork Proctor was the life of the party, as always, and is another one who looks just like he did when he was the Sahara lifeguard in 1956. He is such a charming, funny man. I wish Vassili Sulich had been there. Besides dancing the lead role in the *Folies*, he used to give ballet barre on stage between shows, before he and Nancy Houssels started Nevada Ballet Theatre. Nancy looked so elegant and beautiful, as always. She is such an asset to our city. She was a principal dancer in the *Folies*. Sal Angelica and Roy Schmider each stopped to visit with me. Roy and I used to do commercials together. After Sal did the Folies years ago, he worked in Juliet Prouse's act.

A public relations representative at the Tropicana told me the costumes were being inventoried and boxed for storage on the property. I asked if anybody had tried to buy the show and she said no, adding that the name belonged to the French company in Paris, so I guess anyone could call them.

There isn't much left to say about the death of the *Folies*. I miss it and all the shows like it.

Really, I miss it all. How lucky we were.

with Jerry Jackson

Chapter 44

The Three Damn Monkeys

In reading over the stories I've written about my interesting life, and in thinking about the ones I haven't written, one mysterious theme keeps reoccurring: My incredibly innocent and trusting nature, or my too stupid, will-she-never-learn nature, whichever you prefer.

I have decided the problem is the three monkeys: See No Evil, Speak No Evil, and Hear No Evil. I learned of them in vacation Bible school when I was seven-years-old. He or she must have been a terrific teacher, because that lesson had a huge impact on my thinking process all my life, even now.

I always thought it was evil of me to think that nice man was inviting me to his room or home for immoral purposes. Who was I to judge him like that, or to judge myself now?

Nobody ever lies to me; they are/were just mistaken. An honest mistake no doubt. Judge not lest you be judged turns out to be a constant theme for me.

Gullible is my middle name. I believe everything, even what I read in the newspaper. (Just kidding, Mr. Editor.) I believe even when part of my rational mind is telling me, "This is ridiculous and can't be true." It's a conscious choice to remain sweet and kind. Pollyanna has nothing on me. Haven't many wonderful things started out being hard to believe at first?

Do you know anything about quantum physics? We're building all these enormous superconductors that speed quarks, (tiny flashes or sparks inside an atom), around in opposite circles until they crash into each other. When they collide scientists learn how creation occurs. Physicists years ago discovered that quarks go where the operator of the experiment thinks they are going to go. Isn't that wild? That's what metaphysicians have known for centuries. You become what you think you are. So maybe being a Pollyanna isn't such a bad thing.

I am wealthy because I'm happy with what I have, and I'm grateful to have it. I am wise because I can learn from books and friends. I am healthy because I constantly tell folks I'm healthy as a horse. Could that be why some people call me a horse's ass? Truth is, nobody calls me that, at least that I know of. I just thought it was a funny thing to say. Well, there is that one daughter in law...

I've always been a storyteller. Texans do that. And dressing rooms are such an intrinsic part of being a performer, because that's where we live and become who we are on stage. It's a magic place. We walk in the door as plain girls next door and turn ourselves into beauties, princesses, goddesses. At the Moulin Rouge in Hollywood in particular I was often asked to tell a story as we were making up. My pals Jan and Darlene were always asking me to "tell us a story Betty."

Somehow, they and the others sitting close to us thought my view of the world and no doubt my Texas accent, were amusing. So I obliged and simply told them about my day.

I was always amazed when they laughed at my little stories. I didn't make anything up. Now that I'm old and gray (white actually) I finally know why I was funny. I am a truth teller, and humor is hidden truth.

The truth is that I have plenty of stories left to tell, and I'm still collecting material. So if any of you know of a nice older rich, (of course!) gentleman interested in a starring role in the next chapter of my life, please let me know.

By the way, in April 2010, I was named one of the *Ten Best Showgirls of All Time* by the *Las Vegas Review-Journal*.